DANCING
WITH LIFE

VINCENT TRAVERS OP

© First Published (1996) by
St Martin Apostolate
42 Parnell Square
Dublin 1

Designed by Steven Hope
Typesetting: Steven Hope Design

Printed in Ireland by
ColourBooks Ltd.

CONTENTS

CHAPTER ONE
YOUNG PEOPLE IN CRISIS

1. Life on 42nd Street   18
2. The Street is a Dead End   22
3. Life in a Crisis Centre   25
4. Street Kids - Our Chosen People   29
5. Child Abuse   33
6. Blue Movies   35
7. Eighteen: A Hell Raiser at Home   37

CHAPTER TWO
PEER PRESSURE

1. Parents: The Turbulent Years   41
2. Teenagers: Be Yourself - Not Someone Else   45

CHAPTER THREE
DRUG ABUSE

1. Saying No to Drugs   50
2. Will Power is not Enough   53
3. Key Players against Drugs   55
4. "My Kid is on Drugs"   59

CHAPTER FOUR
SEXUAL MORALITY

1.	Everybody's Not Doing It!	63
2.	What Harm is There if we Love each Other?	65
3.	Why Wait Until After Marriage?	67
4.	Love in Marriage	70

CHAPTER FIVE
A.I.D.S.

1.	A Life and Death Issue	74
2.	A.I.D.S. is a Death Sentence	77
3.	Innocent at Risk	80
4.	Wrecked Beauty	85

CHAPTER SIX
SUICIDE

1.	Suicide – Why?	89
2.	A Tragedy Waiting to Happen	92
3.	A Cry for Help	95
4.	Causes of Suicide	99
5.	Myths and Taboos	103
6.	The Worst has Happened	106
7.	Those Left Behind	110
8.	Teenage Suicides	114

1. A Hell-Hole   122
2. Prisoners are People Too!   126
3. Life Behind Bars   129
4. Is Revenge the Answer?   133
5. Verbal Violence   137
6. Prison Chaplain   141
7. Sea of Stress   145
8. Why More Prisons?   148
9. A Different Prison System   151
10. Dead Man Walking   155
11. Farewell Mountjoy   159

Introduction

This book like every book has a history. It owes its existence to many influences. These were, first the place where I was born, the family I grew up in, the fact that I became a Dominican, but also, and significantly, the places where I worked and the people who became part of my life.

It was never my intention to write a book. I wrote over a period of four years in the family oriented St Martin Magazine and it was the decision of the editorial board to put the articles together in book form. I am as surprised as anyone else to see 'Dancing With Life' in print. I don't claim superior knowledge on the subject matter. If the views I have expressed are to merit consideration it can only be on the basis that I have dealt with these issues in a variety of real life situations.

LISBON

My first assignment was to our priory Corpo Santo, situated on the banks of the river Tagus in Lisbon. The Irish Dominicans first arrived in Portugal during the penal days and have been in residence uninterruptedly, for close on 400 years. In the early years the priory was on the outskirts of the city, but in time old Lisbon like many a city outgrew itself, its centre re-located, and today Corpo Santo is downtown. Oddly enough, it stands in the middle of the "red" light district.

I was given responsibility for Catholic education in two international and non-denominational schools known locally as St Julian's (it followed the English curriculum to A levels) and St Columba's (it followed the American High School system). The students came from a variety of ethnic and cultural backgrounds, and between them represented over thirty nationalities. For eight engaging years, Monday to Friday, we struggled to make sense of the gospel and mysteries of our faith. As a young priest, I was stretched far beyond the boundaries of a theology I had studied in the seminary and the confines of an extremely limited experience of life. Twice weekly, students of all denominations assembled first thing in the mornings in the school hall for common prayer. This was my first experience of ecumenism and it came at a time when it wasn't yet 'proper' or 'respectable' for catholics and protestants to pray together. When I look across the span of life between, I still see in my mind's eye the faces of these young people of the sixties; vibrant, mischievous, awkward, questioning everything, debunking the church and its teachings and, at the same time, seekers of a truth that would set them free to find their space in the world and give meaning and purpose to their lives.

I visited Portugal in the Autumn of '95 and had the great pleasure of meeting old students, now young parents struggling to pass beliefs and values to their children in a world more confused and complicated than the one they grew up in. The young people of St Julian's and St Columba's brought a vision and dimension of life that makes me forever grateful for my Lisbon days.

TRINIDAD

I was, however, ready for a change when my Superior mentioned the West Indies. I left Portugal with 'saudades' for our mission on the beautiful tropical islands of Trinidad and Tobago. I went, almost overnight, from the first world to the third world. I was appointed to a remote parish on the North coast. The little village of Matelot with a population of about five hundred people was the village at the end of the parish and on a road that petered into the sea. The people were poor and life was hard. There were few creature comforts. There was no electricity, no running water, no medical clinic, poor roads that made transportation of fish and vegetables, the only means of livelihood, difficult and, during the wet season, almost impassable and inaccessible to the market place in the capital, Port of Spain.

But not all was gloom and doom. The people, despite

the hardships, had a remarkable sense of humour and a capacity to enjoy life, not just at carnival time but whenever a family or village occasion called for a celebration.

Each day ended on a spectacular note with mother nature putting on a breathtaking display – a glorious sunset like a massive fireball falling slowly and majestically from the sky and disappearing into the deep ocean on the distant horizon. And then the haunting twilight soft and gentle, ushering in the darkness and the long hours of eventide spent in the shade of the hurricane lamp and at the mercy of peevish mosquitoes. It was in many ways a lonely outpost, but one destined to have a profound impact on my life.

I came to the parish at a time when the people were discontented at the hand fate had dealt them. There was a growing sense that life was not fair and did not have to be the way it was: a dawning that if things were to improve it was up to themselves, not outsiders or experts, to be agents of change. People were dreaming of a better life, the winds of change were blowing, and I was caught in the current.

The village council decided it was time to do something and that the best course of action was to bring their plight to the attention of the Prime Minister. A bus was hired. A memorandum outlining grievances was drawn up. The media was briefed. The general public was sensitised to the appalling quality of life on the North Coast. The protest had the desired effect. A delegation of villagers was met by a high ranking official in the Prime Minister's office. The country was shocked. At the end of an eventful day villagers made the journey home feeling immensely relieved and greatly encouraged. Their self-confidence was up. More protests were organised and slowly but surely, the momentum became unstoppable. Things did not change overnight but gradually government was persuaded to act and responded with a development plan for the area.

The Chinese have a saying that a long journey begins when the first step is taken. Unquestionably, for the people of Matelot the bus trip to the Prime Minister's office was that first step, because four years later they saw the transformation in their fortunes, with the installation of electricity, new roads, a medical clinic, a secondary school, revolutionary in nature, because it took into account not just academic standards but local needs and talents. And, most significantly, an increased sense of morale and self-esteem.

The Matelot story became an example to other depressed villages. If you want a better life, you must work hard, take risks and not depend on others to do for you what you can do for yourselves. Word too, reached across the seas to the ears of the Radharc people and inspired them to make a film for Irish Television documenting a rags to riches journey of a small remote village in the third world that dared to stand up for itself and fight the odds.

IRAN

A simple phone call from Dublin brought an end to my life in the Caribbean. The message was simple, "we have a vacancy in Tehran! Would you think about it?"

The Irish Dominican mission to Iran started in 1962. The founding fathers occupied a small dwelling house in the heart of the city. Four years later, they were in a position to negotiate the purchase of a priceless piece of land a few blocks away. It was on this prime site that they built the church and priory of St Abraham's with, in the main, the pennies and shillings donated by the many friends and supporters of the St Martin de Porres Apostolate.

I arrived in Tehran in the late '70's at the height of the oil boom. The Shah of Iran had committed the pedro dollars to a policy of industrial rather than agricultural reforms. Expertise and technology was brought in from different parts of the world to implement the economic plan. The official government line was that foreigners were contributing to the development of the country and welcome. Anti-government forces portrayed the foreign presence as an encroachment of western culture and hostile to Islamic values and beliefs. There was no doubt that Iranians, with some justification, resented the foreign presence and felt threatened by what was perceived to be an evil influence on their culture, customs and traditions. There is, no doubt too, that the enemies of the Shah used the foreign card to great effect in fanning the flames of revolution.

St Abraham's was a unique parish community with parishioners from so many different corners of the world, East and West. But these were difficult times too. The Americans in particular were, unfairly, more hated than anyone else. Indeed, anyone who looked white and spoke English was regarded as American. I'd wake up in the morning and say to myself "I hate this place" and then in the next breath say "but it's fascinating." And it was, painfully so, in being part of a tiny insignificant minority, socially, politically, culturally and spiritually, but despised because of colour and nationality. It wasn't however, without a great learning experience. It gave me a sympathy for minority groups which I didn't have before and one I will hold on to and never let go.

Inevitably, the revolution came. The Shah was overthrown and replaced by a government of Islamic fundamentalists under the leadership of Ahyatolla Komeinei. Inevitably, too, the Irish Dominicans were expelled from Iran, but happily, the authorities never expropriated the property.

TALLAGHT

I returned to Ireland after 17 years overseas to work in the parish of St Mary's, Tallaght. The Tallaght of the midsixties was a rural village with a population of 250 families, nestled in the foothills of the Dublin mountains. City planners had earmarked the surrounding area as a site for a new satellite town. By the early '80's St Mary's had developed into the fastest growing parish in Western Europe and was now part of greater Dublin.

Nothing, from a pastoral point of view, could have been more exciting or challenging. The parish was made up of young families of hard working parents with dreams and hopes, sparing no effort to give their children the best possible start in life. I marvel still as I remember the seemingly boundless energy of so many people, young and old, who unselfishly created a multiplicity of organisations to meet the social, educational, health, artistic and recreational needs of a growing population. It is what we make out of what we have, not what we are given, that separates one person from another. Tallaght of the '70's and '80's is a tale demanding to be told. I was part of it for six years and they remain the most enriching years of my priesthood.

NEW YORK

The two years I spent working with street kids happened by accident, or should I say was an act of divine providence. I was all set to do a six months pastoral course in the States when a chance meeting with a colleague reading the New Yorker changed the direction in which I was heading. There was an article describing the work of a crisis centre for street kids and I knew in a flash that that is where I should be, working in the field, rather than studying in a classroom. I made enquiries as to my suitability. I was called for inter-view and invited to join the staff and two weeks after finish-ing in Tallaght I started my first day in the centre.

G.K. Chesterton once defined genius as the power to observe the obvious. I soon discovered that the centre was a great school in the 'obvious'. I learned in a new way a truth we have all been brought up on, that everyone has inside himself – what shall I call it – a piece of good news, a core of decency, an inner light, a spark of the divine. The street kids had their way of expressing it and resorted to it only after they had hit rock bottom and the only way left was up . . . or out. They would say "Don't Dis me, man" – don't disrespect me. And it's true that what we need more than anything else is respect. Equally true, when you give respect, you get respect, perhaps not at once but, eventually, you do.

The respect we owe the dignity of the human person, as a unique and precious work of God, is at the root of all moral behaviour, fairness, honesty, courtesy, tolerance and justice. Nobody is excused from the duty of respect, because the other person is in trouble or has a different colour, back-ground, lifestyle, speaks a different language, goes to a dif-ferent Church, or because he/she is too young or old or weak to defend themselves. A person is a person no matter how small. The great law of respect commands that no one is written off as no good or incapable of change.

I left the centre at 11.30 on a winter's night in late January for my home at St Vincent Ferrer's on Lexington Avenue. The rain was pouring down. The wind went through you for a short cut. It was a night to be indoors. The Broadway shows were over and theatre-goers had returned to their homes or hotels. I never saw Times Square so deserted. As I walked along Broadway a young woman stepped out of a doorway and asked if I would like some company. I said:

"No, thank you very much."

"We could share the same umbrella?"

"No, thank you very much."

"We could go to your place?"

"No, thank you very much."

"We could go to my place?"

"No, thank you very much."

I was extremely uncomfortable. Usually people did not persist. She continued to walk alongside. We were almost but not quite sharing the same umbrella! We reached a pedestrian crossing. The red light flashing a "Don't Walk" signal. At this point she turned and said rather caustically: "Tell me, who are you 'Mr. No thank you very much'?" I decided to level with her and replied: "I'm a Catholic Priest."

She looked at me disbelievingly and said with a wry smile: "So you're a reverend Father?"

"Yes."

"Well if you're a reverend Father, I'm a reverend mother."

The light changed to green and signalled "go" and together we moved, side by side for a couple of blocks, until we came to a halt at another pedestrian red light. Again she looked, this time dismissively and said:

"Good night reverend Father."

I could not resist:

"Good night reverend mother."

We crossed the road in-step and walked in silence. At some moment I sensed a change of mood. Suddenly, she stopped, so did I, tears were running down her cheeks. Very gently she said:

"Father. please pray for me."

I nodded and said:

"Yes, provided you pray for me."

Neither of us spoke again. At that moment she was not a prostitute and I was not a priest. We were two human beings meeting for a brief moment at the crossroads of life. Quietly she turned and walked into the night and I continued home. I never saw her again on the streets of Times Square and I've never forgotten her.

MOUNTJOY

I have written at some length of my experiences as a prison chaplain in Mountjoy prison. There is, however, one important aspect I omitted which I believe is important and, interestingly enough, relates to a feature of work in New York, which likewise, I did not dwell on.

The centre ran an educational outreach programme to High Schools in Brooklyn, Bronx, Harlem, and other areas in and beyond the New York area. On the basis, that prevention is better than cure, the bottom line was always the same. If you have problems at home the street is no place to solve them; there isn't time. Running away adds to the problems. We were not telling them to stay in a situation that was hopeless or dangerous. We offered alternatives to the street, and the help to face problems without running away from them.

The fact that a speaker could begin his presentation with the statement: "I work full time with street kids" commanded attention. He had credibility. The audience was listening.

Shortly after I took up my position in Mountjoy I was invited to speak on prison to the 6th formers in the Dominican Secondary School, Griffith Avenue. It was impossible to separate prison from the reasons why people end up in prison. In a curious way, I found I was discussing the very issues that dominated the talks I gave in New York: child abuse, substance and alcohol abuse, blue movies, A.I.D.S., suicide, poverty, peer pressure, family relationships, personal responsibility, integrity and related subjects.

More invitations followed from other schools and also from a variety of adult groups. When I was introduced as a

prison chaplain I had a captive audience. I wasn't saying anything new or radical. I was, however, using prison as a medium of communication. I was using it as a kind of filter to focus
on issues of grave concern to parents, teachers and teenagers,
and this angled approach, coloured what I was saying, caught
the eye and held the attention. In 'Dancing With Life' I'm
using the same medium, covering the same material, wearing
the same variety of hats; 'Prison', 'Street,' 'Teacher', 'Pastor',
and hoping to produce the same effects. Perhaps, what I'm
about, can be best summed up in story form.

I invited a group of 40 Leaving certificate girls and their
teachers to come and see Mountjoy from the inside. The highlight was the visit to the women's prison. The encounter took
place in the yard. The girls were totally ill at ease. The
inmates were in control. This was their territory. They came
across as intimidating. But things are not always as they
appear. It was up to me to break the ice. I made the intro-
ductions, I told the inmates about the talk I gave in the school
and my regret at not having one of them to share their prison
experience. I then added: "Now is your chance."

What followed was riveting. Nothing was said that these
young women hadn't heard before from parents and teachers,
but in the bleak prison surroundings it sounded powerful.
The inmates spoke with authority. It came from the heart.
Here are some of the things they said: "Don't do drugs. They
are stupid. They destroy the body and the sound mind that
God and our parents have given us." "Stay off the booze. It
will wreck your head." "Stay in school. Work hard. You are
going nowhere unless you do your best."

"Don't stay out at night."

"Listen to your Ma, Da."

"Don't be a copy-cat. Don't give your power away."

"Don't mess with life or you'll end up like us."

The girls were spellbound. I, too, was captivated. The
message was simple. Life is worth living, because we have so
much to live for. But, life is short, so why risk making it short-
er? Why dice with death when we can dance with life?

CHAPTER ONE

Young People in Crisis

1. Life on 42nd Street

2. The Street is a Dead End

3. Life in a Crisis Centre

4. Street Kids – Our Chosen People

5. Child Abuse

6. Blue Movies

7. Eighteen: A Hell Raiser at Home

1   *Life on 42nd Street*

The last official function I performed as Parish Priest of Tallaght in January 1985 was to co-sign a document with the late Archbishop of Dublin, Kevin McNamara, whereby, at the stroke of a pen, the parish of St. Mary's became four parishes.

Two days later, I was a passenger on board an Aer Lingus Jumbo Jet, flying to New York to take up an appointment as a full time worker in a crisis centre for street kids under 21 in the Times Square area of the city.

40 DEUCE

I will always remember the first day in the centre. I still vividly recall walking down the infamous W42nd Street – street kids call it 40 deuce – at 7.30 in the morning. Every depravity man is capable of creating was on sale. Little did I realise that the thriving sex industry and drug pushing operating on 42nd Street and Times Square would be an occupational hazard I would face day and night for the next two years.

I was feeling quite apprehensive as I approached the centre, wondering to myself, if I had, in fact, made the right decision in volunteering for this special kind of work. Nothing in Tallaght or in my past had prepared me for this undertaking.

When I stepped inside the reception area, I was surprised to hear a familiar accent. It was the voice of a 15 year old black boy. I asked him where he came from originally. He said, "The West Indies." I asked, "Which Island?" He said, "Trinidad." I enquired, "Which part?" He said, "Toco." Toco is located on the North Coast of the Island and is so remote that locally it is known as 'behind God's back". I was Parish Priest in Toco from 1971 to 1976. I asked him his name and date of birth. When he answered, I realised to my amazement, that he was one of the first babies I had baptised. He and his family left Trinidad four years later and emigrated to New York City. In 1976 I was transferred to our Dominican mission in Iran and from there I came to Tallaght in 1979 and then to New York in 1985.

In the intervening years his life moved in one direction and mine in another. Then, in an extraordinary turn of events, our paths crossed unexpectedly in a crisis centre off 42nd Street, and I found myself helping him to turn his life around, think and feel good things about himself, and walk away from a destructive lifestyle that was slowly destroying him.

Whatever misgivings I had about my suitability for working with street kids, the meeting with that young man from the past dissipated my anxieties and convinced me that this new chapter in my life was meant to be. Now, when I look back across the years, I realise that in New York I was singularly blessed.

KIDS ON THE RUN

I plan, on the basis of that experience, to write on the problems of homeless youths, life in the street, the programme we operated, how it helped to redirect many young lives away from the streets towards a more productive life; the lessons we can learn, especially when dealing with young people in crisis.

Young people are running away from home in greater numbers. Despite the seriousness of the problem, surprisingly little is known about this phenomenon. Homeless youths are one of the shadow populations of our society. Much about their lifestyle and means of support is unknown. Even less is known about how to deal with their specific needs and problems.

IMPORTANT DISTINCTIONS

It is important, at the outset, to make some distinctions that may help towards a better understanding of the homeless and runaway youths.

Young people who run away from home are not street
people. While some may become such, the mere fact of running away does not make one a street kid. Indeed, only a
fraction of those who run away become street persons.
Neither should we consider the children of homeless families to be street persons, although these are not far from slip-
ping into that category.

Neither are young homeless adults, temporarily living
rough because of some unexpected economic or family circumstances, to be considered street persons.

There are, also, dreamers, seekers after the truth, who by
reason of – to us – an irresponsible lifestyle are incorrectly
labelled 'drifters'. They do not, as I understand it, fall into
the category of street persons.

What is an authentic 'street person'? Put very simply, he
is one who has definitely severed his relationship with his
family and now relates primarily to the street and his street
family. He is someone who is disconnected not only from his
family but from other nurturing institutions in society:
neighbourhood, school, church, career opportunities and
from almost all healthy adult relationships.

VICTIMS

Those who came to us in 42nd Street were, on the whole,
victims of failed families and failed parents, victims of abuse,
physical and sexual, victims, too, of spiritual and emotional
neglect.

If I were to describe the profile of a typical street kid's
family, it would go something like this: The family has
almost always ceased to exist, because of divorce or separa-
tion. What remained was usually headed by a single parent,
generally female, frequently never married, trapped in the
lower end of the social ladder who is beset by economic difficulties and hardships and is utterly dependant on public
assistance for survival.

Sadly only 16% of the young men and women who came
to the centre returned home permanently. Even more tragically, only 16% returned home to a two parent family.

One of the saddest conclusions to which I reluctantly came is that many of these families and their children could have coped with the demands of life in a simpler and primitive society. Unfortunately, the fast lane, the often chaotic pace of modern life, and the breakdown of moral and cultural values, constitute a poor, even hostile, environment in which only the strongest families flourish.

2 The Street is a Dead End

Why so many young people today are running away from home is not altogether clear. It is not a simple issue. Contrary to the popular myth that these youths are running to the 'Big City' for adventure and excitement, the reality is that many are running from family problems and conflicts. We read about the adventures of Mark Twain's 'Huckleberry Finn' and begin to wonder how many are inspired by his example. We forget Huckleberry Finn was an abused child. He ran from an alcoholic father who frequently beat him up.

RUNNING FROM NOT RUNNING TO

Many homeless youths are running not *to* something but *from* bad experiences, namely: physical and sexual abuse, a family that is uninvolved, uncaring or pre-occupied, over-crowding, poor housing, unemployment, a sense of failure. Some are not able to give a reason for leaving, other than a feeling of being disconnected from their families. There are, of course, the irresponsible few who are out of control and simply want to do their own thing however outrageous or bizarre, and regardless of the consequences. The varying reasons cited for leaving home do not seem to fall onto any clear pattern, especially when it is recognised that many more of such youths, faced by similar problems, do not leave home.

The homeless young men and women under 21 years that I met in the crisis centre in New York City came from every socio-economic group: White, Black, Hispanic, Asian, male and female, innocent and streetwise. Those who came from upper income families were few in number. Slightly more came from middle class families. The vast majority came from poor disadvantaged families.

TOUGHEST IN THE WORLD

The centre was residential. On any given day there was an average of 250. About 60% were young men and 40% young women. There was a special floor to cater for mothers and babies. These were not the toughest kids in New York, but reputedly, the toughest in the world. Some were amongst the most damaged young people I have met.

Some were so far down the road in crime, drug addiction, prostitution, chaotic lifestyles that, barring divine intervention, the journey back to reality and normal living was simply beyond them. Half of them were so sad and desolate that they tried to kill themselves or thought seriously about it. One third were helped to rebuild their lives and start all over again. Tragically, the rest will, in time, die horrible deaths in the streets.

When homeless youths go on the streets, the first reaction may be a sense of exhilaration and freedom. But fairly soon, after experiencing the harsh reality of survival away from home, there are second thoughts. Invariably, they return home and life resumes again even though problems with their families stay unresolved. Old pressures build up and in a matter of weeks or months they find themselves back on the streets. This process can repeat itself several times until they reach the point of feeling that there is no hope of reconciling family differences and that their future lies elsewhere.

Usually they come to the centre as a last resort, because they have nowhere else to go and are tired of running.

TRYING TO SURVIVE

About 60% were involved in prostitution. Of course, they tried to hide from themselves what was actually going on in their lives. They did not see themselves as prostitutes. They called this activity 'making a few bucks'.

In the beginning a girl would say "Father, I'm no prostitute. He isn't a pimp. He's my boyfriend and he needs me". In the beginning!

In the beginning a boy would say "Father, I'm not gay. I'm not a hustler. I'm just trying to stay alive." In the beginning!

But after two or three months of this way of life it becomes increasingly difficult to separate what you are from what you do. You become what you do and you no longer care.

The girls show it first in their faces. The boys can hide it longer. But the boys "die" sooner. The girls survive longer. It is simply more acceptable for a girl to work the streets than for a boy.

On the outside, they are streetwise and tough, but inside, scarred and needy. They are no different from their peers in their desire to be loved and cared for and given the opportunity to grow up, get a job and live decent respectable lives. But life has dealt them a heavy blow from which some, sadly, never recover.

STREET NO PLACE FOR YOUNG

So they have made the street their home. But the street cannot take care of them. It is full of danger. It is a hard and hostile world and gives nothing back to those who have made it their own. The street imprisons them. It is a dead end. It is no place for the young to solve their problems.

3 Life in a Crisis Centre

Many of the street kids, 21 years and under, who came to the Crisis Centre, made you wonder if there was anything anyone could do to help them. Often the answer was devastatingly frank and brutal; no one could because they had lost the courage to live and had stopped believing that tomorrow could be better.

Nonetheless, we had a really good programme for those who could take it. It is worth describing in some detail. It was not designed overnight, it took years to develop. I believe we can learn from it and apply the insights in helping young people in crisis today at home or in school.

STREET CODE

Life in the street is harsh and bleak. The street code is simple and cruel. Exploit or be exploited. Intimidate or be intimidated. Seduce or be seduced. Do unto others before they do unto you. Survive or die. Some do not learn fast enough about survival. Others do not know how to survive anywhere else. What they are living is a nightmare, a real horror story, easier to imagine than describe.

OPEN INTAKE

We operated a policy of open intake 24 hours a day, 7 days a week, because we recognised how vulnerable the young are and how dangerous the street is. No one was turned away on a first visit. No one had to justify needs. Open intake means being able to say: "We're glad you're here. Please stay. Don't go away. If you stay we will do our best to treat you with respect and ask you to treat us in the same way".

It also means saying: "Don't bring the street in here. Leave lying, cheating, bullying, manipulation outside."

Policies are spelled out in language that is clear and simple. No weapons. No drugs. No alcohol. No physical violence. No verbal abuse. No physical contact.

At first, I was puzzled by the policy of no physical contact. It seemed puritanical and old fashioned. But I quickly came to appreciate the wisdom behind it. The young men and women are in serious crisis. The priority is to help them regain control of their lives again. Clearly, this was not the time to be emotionally involved.

Personal relationships could only distract from their immediate goal. Now was the time to focus attention and energies on solving their problems. Nothing must stand in the way. When the crisis was over, there would be all the time in the world for falling in love and entering into normal and healthy human relationships.

LINE ON THE SAND

There was a 9.30p.m. curfew policy. This made huge demands on the activities of the young people accustomed to roaming the streets at all hours of the night. Amazingly, on any given night only a handful went AWOL. Here we have, clearly illustrated, a truth that, today, seems forgotten. Young people need limits, lines drawn in the sand, that state this far and no further. Parents and teachers ignore this truth at their peril.

END OF THE DAY

At 9.30 a light supper snack was served followed by a general assembly for residents and staff in the main living room. This nightly gathering provided the opportunity to identify and address conflicts and issues that may have occurred during the day.

Questions were asked and answered: disputes and arguments aired and settled. There were words of support for those doing well and encouragement for those struggling. The aim was to create a positive frame of mind for the day ahead and ensure that no one went to bed feeling bad or mad. These were precious moments in the daily life of the centre: the time when the so called trouble-makers, the no-hopers, the lost generation, pondered the events of the day, their own particular journey and story. Fittingly, the day concluded with night prayer in an atmosphere of peace and quiet.

HYGIENE

Great emphasis was placed on personal hygiene. During the hours of darkness each kid's clothing was laundered by night staff. The new day began with a 7.00a.m. wake-up call. A shower was obligatory. Breakfast was served in the cafeteria and by 9.00a.m. each was expected to be on his way. Looking clean and smelling good and ready to take on their particular business of the day.

There is, I believe, a definite co-relation between dirt and violence. A dirty centre is an argumentative one. A filthy home, school, theatre, restaurant, communicates chaos and a couldn't care less attitude. You feel devalued in that kind of setting.

The centre was kept spotlessly clean. If graffiti appeared on the wall, they were immediately washed away. The interior was furnished with good taste. Warm coloured carpets, brightly painted walls, beautiful paintings on the walls, plants, flowers and comfortable furniture all combined to communicate a sense that people count and that this is a good place to be.

COMMITMENT TO CHANGE

The centre existed for the street kids. The programme was structured to make it as easy as possible to succeed. Every effort was made to help each one develop an appropriate plan of action aimed at getting his life together again. A commitment to a change of life was a condition of residency.

ACTIONS HAVE CONSEQUENCES

Anyone who deliberately sabotaged this plan was discharged, on the principle that actions have consequences.

Discharge, however, was not a first option but a last resort. Clearly, it was in no one's interest to support negative or destructive behaviour. The irresponsible youth, not the centre, was accountable for the discharge. The line was: "Sorry, but its over for now. You did not honour your commitments. You are not ready yet for the services we offer". He would be referred to a homeless shelter and invited to return after 30 days and try again. There was no limit on the number of times he could return provided he was under 21 years of age.

The miracle is that we succeeded in helping to salvage one third of our population to rebuild their broken lives. Sadly the other two thirds will eventually die horrible deaths in the streets.

4 *Street Kids – Our Chosen People*

He was a typical Times Square street kid. Not the type you would want to meet in a dark lane at night. Rather, the type you would want to have with you, if you had to walk down that lane.

He was tired of sleeping in the subways and doing things that made him feel bad about himself. He had heard about the Crisis Centre off 42nd Street and decided to check the place out for himself.

He sat down on a chair opposite me. It was late at night. His eyes were a vivid blue, intensely alive and watchful. I noticed that he didn't blink very often and would carefully look away for a moment and then just as carefully look back again. I marvelled that such a young man's face could be so ravaged and old.

"My name is Vincent", I said. "Mine is Mario", he said. We shook hands. He had a man's hand in a boy's body.

" I left home when I was 12" he said, with a flat finality in his voice. "My mother had a drinking problem. My father was a violent man. I've been in the streets too long. I'm only 16 and I have a drugs and alcohol problem." "What have you been on?" I asked. "Everything" he said, "but mostly crack." I said "Stay with us for a while, give us a chance to help you." He looked away carefully breaking eye contact for a moment, and then just as carefully looked back. "You don't blink very much." he said suspiciously. I said "I don't when I'm concentrating." There was a short pause. He seemed to be weighing up the pros and cons and then, slowly with each word precisely measured said, "OK, I'll give it a shot. I'll take it one day at a time."

How do you begin to help someone like Mario change the whole course of his life? I'd like to tell you about the programme we ran to help street kids like Mario believe in themselves, and believe, too, that tomorrow could be different.

THE PROGRAMME

The under 21's who came through our doors off the mean New York streets were in deep crisis. Every effort was made to meet basic needs. If he was hungry we fed him. If he needed a shower, he got one. If he needed clean clothes we gave him a change of clothing. If he was suffering from sexually transmitted diseases, malnutrition, drug or alcohol abuse, or simply run down, he saw the doctor in the medical unit. If he was in trouble with the law, he saw one of the lawyers in the legal unit. Their needs were real and varied, hence a wide variety of services were available. In responding immediately we were loving them in practical ways and, hoping, as a result, they could begin to love themselves tomorrow.

SECURITY

We offered sanctuary – protection from the horrors of the street and their past. Armed guards were on duty around the centre 24 hours a day, 7 days a week, not to keep the street kids in but to keep pimps, drug pushers, and undesirable people out. Protection is very important. Young people can only grow and develop in an environment where they feel safe and secure. Street life is chaotic. A street kid seldom knows where he will get his next meal or sleep that night. We provided structure and stability without a lot of rules and regulations. This approach alleviated a lot of anxiety and facilitated the constructive use of time and energy.

STRUCTURE

Structure is for the sake of choice. Within 24 hours of admission or, as soon as it was feasible, we sat down with each individual – and with his family if that was possible – for an in-depth discussion on what he would like to do with his life. This, one to one, gave us the opportunity to convey a sense that someone cares and there is a future for him.

CHOICE

Choice is the principle of change. We encouraged him to make good choices. We guided him step by step, firmly but gently, to formulate a life plan that was appropriate to his needs and within his capabilities. We helped him to discriminate between what was possible and practical, and to identify the steps he would have to take to realise his plan. We wanted him to succeed, while he was with us, and after he left us.

TEAM WORK

Once the plan of action was drawn up it was presented for evaluation to the staff team of group leaders, counsellors, social workers, doctor, nurse, psychiatrist, lawyer and chaplain at the daily case review.

The collective wisdom of the team was drawn upon to assess the strengths and weaknesses of the plan. Nothing was left to chance.

FOLLOW PLAN

Changes were made if this was seen to be in his best interest. The plan, modified or unchanged, was brought back to the young man for his response. He had his final say. Once his approval was given the plan was sacrosanct. It could not be changed either by himself or his counsellor without the permission of the team. It had to be followed. In this way, a process of accountability was set in motion between the young man and his counsellor and between the counsellor and the team. Progress was monitored. Each street kid was obliged to sit down with his counsellor each evening for a review of the day. These were precious moments. A time to listen and learn, give encouragement or praise, ask for more if more of an effort was called for, share experiences and, most of all, build relationships.

If a young man was 18 years and could not return home, his plan would be independent living. This would involve job search, finding suitable employment, opening a savings account in the centre by lodging 75% of his weekly pay cheque.

If all goes according to plan he would, after seven or eight weeks of employment, have enough money saved to be in a position to rent an apartment and support himself. A planned discharge from the centre would be put into effect. If however, he had a drug or alcohol problem, the plan would be placement in a rehabilitation programme.

HARD WORK

The programme was good, but if the young man or woman does not put in the effort, he or she is not going to get anything out of it. Of course, rejected, exploited and undisciplined youths cannot be expected to make serious and dramatic changes in their lives all at once. Rome was not built in a day. We did not expect instant miracles. Since they are not with us very long, often it is not possible to effect massive changes in their livestyles. As long as they were serious and sincere in following their plans, they were welcome to stay. If they can work it out in a day, that is what we will help them to do. If it takes a couple of months, then they will stay for that period of time.

Unfortunately, not all succeed. Some are not capable of taking the structure of the programme. Some cannot relate to a lifestyle of responsibility. Some cannot respond to people who care.

Some lose hope that the future can be better. And so they leave. Maybe they'll come back. If they do, we'll be there for them.

STREET KIDS – OUR CHOSEN PEOPLE

It is a law of life that we do not relate to institutions or institutional theories. We respond to people, and best of all to people who love us for our own sakes with no strings attached.

The philosophy of the centre was based on Covenant Love. "Covenant " is a biblical word. Behind it is a wonderful idea. It expresses the special bond between God and his people. We are his chosen people and He loves us unconditionally and without reservation.

We respond to the street kids within the context of Covenant Love. We commit ourselves to accepting each of them as a precious, invaluable human being. Covenant Love is a love that is consistent and personal. A love that challenges and confronts but is never withdrawn.

Street kids are our "chosen people".

5 *Child Abuse*

For two years (1985-1987) I had to deal with the child abuse scene on a day to day basis in a crisis centre in New York City. I am neither shocked nor dismayed by it. I am, however, deeply concerned. The more this abuse is brought out of the closet and into the open, the more we are protecting and defending innocent victims.

SEX OBJECTS

Many people find it hard to believe that children are sex objects and that adults abuse them to satisfy their sexual needs. Consequently, thousands of children suffer from the traumatic effects of sexual abuse for the rest of their lives.

Perhaps I can comment on this tragedy by sharing a conversation I had in the centre with a sexually abused teenager. She said: "Why did my father do that stuff to me? What made him be like that to me? Why me?"

I said: "Often people who abuse children sexually and physically were abused themselves when they were little. The abused becomes the abuser."

"Sometimes adults who are disappointed or unfulfilled by adult sex seem to think they can, through children, return to their adolescence. That was a period when sex was new and unspoiled and so sexual interaction with children makes them feel excited again. It makes them feel powerful."

We do not know enough about incest and child molesting but work goes on. It happens a lot more than people will admit. . . almost as bad as the experience itself is carrying the burden of guilt inside you.

THE PAIN OF IT

I can still see her sitting in the chair opposite me. She

had that frightened far-away look. For a ling time she did
not say a word. I honoured the silence. I looked into her
face. Pain stared out at me.

"He made me do things, I feel dirty, I feel guilty."
"It wasn't you, it was he. You just happened to be in the
wrong place at the wrong time."
"My mother caught us."
"She caught him not you."
"She blamed me. She called me a whore."
"Your mother was wrong. It's his problem. Not yours."

The child abuser is a human being, desperately in need
of help too. Sadly, he discovers that being the abuser can be
a gratifying experience. Usually, he feels sexually inadequate with adults. With children he feels, more in control,
more in charge. It's a power thing. Sadly, too, the help he
most urgently needs is seldom available.

FOREWARNED

Children can be abused inside or outside the home, and
must be warned about this terrible possibility. Warned, not
just about the complete stranger, but that someone very
important and close to the family, can do bad things to them.
Parents should tell their kids to yell and scream if someone
tries to touch them, makes them feel funny, tells them to keep
it a secret, not to tell Mom or Dad, or threatens them in any
way if they tell. Tell them clearly, "We want to know, we'll
be glad you told us." I could say more but, perhaps, enough
has been said to heighten awareness of this tragic problem.
Should you have some reasons for suspecting an incident of
child abuse you have a moral obligation to report it without
delay to the proper authorities.

6 *Blue Movies*

There are many reasons why there is a sex industry. None of the reasons are mysterious. The simple fact is that people want one. The reasons are the same: greed and lust. Their greed, namely those who promote and support the industry; our lust and our inability to care what happens to young women and young men, whose lives and spirits are damaged almost beyond the point of repair.

SICK AND SAVAGE INDUSTRY

There are countless people, here and abroad, who patronise this million dollar industry and make a lot of ruthless and unwholesome people very rich. Each time we hire a blue movie from a video club and show it on our television screens, we support and tolerate this very sick and savage industry that treats young people as merchandise to be bought and sold and subjected to every perversion that man can create.

Millions believe the bizarre myth that prostitution is nothing more than a commercial "fun" transaction. We have in our supposedly liberated society, chosen to identify sex with entertainment and to scoff at the notion that there is something sacred and deeply personal, private and intimate about sexual pleasure. Prostitution and pornography reduce sex to something vulgar and coarse. It is without humour or humanity.

I wince with dismay at the idea of parents bringing blue movies into their homes. I shudder at the thought of boys and girls, hardly in their teens, having easy access to these films in the sanctuary of their homes. I have seen the almost irreversible damage pornography can do to our ability to enter into and form or maintain wholesome human relationships.

EVIL

I don't buy into the arguments about the harmlessness of pornography. Frankly, I have lost patience with that kind of argument. I have lost all patience since the time I have lived and worked with street kids in New York city. At any time we had two hundred and fifty kids living in the centre. Most of them were victims of the Times Square/West 42nd Street sex industry. It's because I know the victims that I have so little patience with those who call pornography a victimless crime.

INNOCENT VICTIMS

Why do you think we send our children to good schools? Why are we so careful about what our children read? Is it because we know that people can be taught good things and we know that they can be taught bad things? We know that, since Adam and Eve. To proclaim self righteously that there is no demonstrative relationship between pornography, violence and warped attitudes, is really ludicrous and ridiculous.

I don't want to enter into serious discussions with these people. I don't think they're intellectually honest. No one who has ever maintained that position has ever come into contact with the victims of pornography and prostitution.

7 *Eighteen: A Hell Raiser at Home*

I was in a deep sleep when the phone rang at 1.30 in the morning. At the other end of the line there was a distraught parent, his voice bordering on desperation, as he described the bizarre behaviour of his 18 year old son. "He's ruining his life. He's wrecking the family. And he's coming between me and my wife. He's out of control. I have locked him out and he's raising hell and threatening to break down the door if I don't let him in."

In due course, I came to know the parents of the young man. They were decent, respectable and caring people, wanting only the best for their son; not monsters, locking him out in the cold. But they were, also, frightened, ashamed, and guilty, seeing the way their son was turning out. They had lost confidence in themselves and wanted to know "where they had gone wrong?"

COMPROMISED

The young man in question is a young adult not a minor! Even so, what parents in their right senses would want to put their own flesh and blood out of the home, however irrational and irresponsible his or her behaviour may be? For most parents, the initial thought of confronting their precious, rebellious child seems frightening. If they fear their son is running wild, starting to live a desperate life of drug addiction or crime, they will want, at all costs, to keep him home where they think he is safe. They will want to avoid rocking the boat by making demands in case they break the slender threads that bind them together as a family.

And yet, if you think about it, parents who tolerate behaviour that is intolerable are, perhaps, without realising it, maintaining and supporting a cruel and destructive lifestyle that is in fact breaking up the home and destroying personal relationships.

GONE TOO FAR

I believe there comes a time when parents in this awful predicament must risk losing a son or daughter, terrible as the prospect is. When they must set limits on what is acceptable and unacceptable behaviour. When they must say: thus far and no further.

They take this risk when saying: "Our home and family are worth coming home to, not because you are in crisis and need a place to live, but because we love you and value you. If you want to be a real member of this family, this is what you have to do."

There is a vast difference between love and approval. Love requires that we distinguish between the person (who is good) and his behaviour (not always good). This is an important distinction because it allows us to say unconditionally and without reservation, "I love you always, and forever, no matter what." and at the same time to say, "It's your ugly, obnoxious behaviour and attitude I disapprove of and hate." To put it simply, love is always unconditional, approval, however is conditional.

So it's alright for parents and children to have differences. It's alright to disagree. It's alright to say, "Johnny I think you are wrong. I regret what you are doing. I still love you nonetheless", and to say, "You have the second last word, but as long as you live under our roof, I have the last."

Young people need discipline. Discipline is a special kind of love. It says, "Johnny, we care, and because we care we are not letting you do as you please."

HIS CHOICE

In this way parents are, agonisingly, asking their son to choose between family life and the outrageous life he is living. Should he continue his destructive lifestyle, then he is choosing to live outside the home. He, not his parents, is putting himself out on the street! In this way, too, parents can get to the point when they can painfully accept his choice, even if it means the loss of a loved one, hopefully only for the time being.

Some young people can be tough and resourceful. They may be far down the road and hard to stop. Sometimes it takes years until they are tired of it all and are ready to stop their negative and outrageous behaviour.

OPEN DOOR

Invariably, when a son makes the first move back to a healthy life, parents will bend over backwards in welcoming him home and going the extra mile. Unfortunately, there are some young people who never learn and never change.

Clearly they have no right to disrupt family life and to cause a rift between parents. At 18 years, they have the right to live outside the home, should they or indeed their parents so decide.

PERSONAL RESPONSIBILITY

It is essential that we try to develop answers to stop the destruction of young lives. True, some troublesome youths may be diagnosed neurotic, psychotic, a victim of child abuse or suffering from poor self-esteem. Others, however, are acting unreasonably and irresponsibly and sometimes parents and professionals do not know what to do.

TOUGH LOVE

Looking for the cause of problems is not enough, if it is blinding us to the real issue that actions have consequences. Without a real focus on personal responsibility by blaming parents and authority figures and the world we live in, we may be ignoring the central issue and thereby wasting precious time and resources. With all respect we need to move more and more in the direction of insisting that young people accept full responsibility for their negative actions. Moreover, we need to provide tough but loving solutions for contemporary problems.

Edmund Burke gives food for thought when he says: "In a free society, for evil to prevail, all that is necessary is that good people do nothing.".

CHAPTER TWO

Peer Pressure

1.   Parents : The Turbulent Years

2.   Teenagers: Be Yourself – Not Someone Else

1 *Parents: The Turbulent Years*

There are many stories told regarding Mark Twain. Here is one I especially like. It appears that Twain, while talking to a friend one day, remarked: "When I was 14, I was thoroughly ashamed of my father. To me, he seemed the dumbest person I had ever come into contact with. But, when I was 21, I was amazed how much the old man had learned in 7 years."

The story is a roundabout way of saying that adolescence is a time of change and uncertainty, when a youth is trying to figure out who he is and what he wants to be; an in-between stage, when he is no longer a child and not yet an adult. It is a time of growth and development when he must adjust to radical changes in his body, outgrow childish emotions and begin to deal with the complexities and responsibilities of adult life.

DIFFICULT TIME

It is a time, too, when youngsters put enormous pressure on themselves. When they desperately want to be successful, and independent of their elders. Some do all kinds of foolish things to get attention. When they move in the fast lane, sometimes the wheels come off. The need to be part of the group motivates them more, perhaps, than anything else.

It's a tough world for the young and the restless to grow up in and an unenviable time for parents. Some understanding of the dynamics of peer pressure is essential if family relationships are to survive the turbulent years of adolescence.

INFLUENCE

There are certain forces at play which must be recognised and respected. Parents need to understand and accept that their children are at an age when the important people in their lives are their friends. Friends are the people who have the strongest hold. This phase will pass, of course, hopefully very quickly. But while they are going through it, it is important to remember that friends, by and large, have the greatest influence, more so than parents, more so perhaps than any other adult.

Parents, have, somehow, got to appreciate the horrible dilemma their youngsters sometimes find themselves in. Any attempt to declare war on their ideas or behaviour may result in being shut out. Parents risk losing their children when they put them in the position of deciding which is the more important, belonging to the family or belonging to the group. These are the years when parents are skating on very thin ice in their relationships with their children. So forcing a teenager to choose between family or friends is thoughtless and basically unhelpful.

I am emphatically, not saying that parents let everything go. I am saying that the young need to feel that their parents at least understand their predicament of wanting to be loyal to family and friends at the same time. I am saying any breakdown in communication, at a time when the young need their parents most of all, is unfortunate and regrettable.

FORMATION

How can parents prepare their teenage sons and daughters to deal with peer pressure and make good decisions at this most difficult stage of their lives? How can they empower their children to cope successfully with drugs, alcohol, smoking, sex, staying out late at night-time, doing their own thing, and the popular belief that "it cannot happen to me"?

What does a parent say when a son or daughter protests: "But Mom, everyone is doing it!" "But Dad, Johnny's father lets him do it, why can't I!" "But Mom, Susie stays out until 2a.m. why can't I?"

I have told the following story so often that soon I'll start believing it myself. But it is true nonetheless, if you understand what I mean! It illustrates how difficult it must be for parents and their teenage children at this stage of life.
Son: "May I have a bike?"

Parent: "Do we look like we can afford a bike?"
Son: "But Johnny has a bike."
Parent: "So if Johnny has diarrhoea, would you want it too?"

While many parents feel powerless to make a difference, they are still in a position to influence and help their kids, especially pre-teens, to resist negative peer pressure.

REAL SAY
Here are some of the things you can do:

1. Get to know your child on a one to one. To really know his concerns, you need to listen every day. Give him the whole of your attention. You need to understand, not just hear. Parents who make that extra effort can exercise a huge influence in their childrens lives.

2. Get him to face his fears. It can be intimidating to be different, to risk ridicule or loss of friends. Help diffuse your child's fears by explaining the possible outcomes of his or her actions. For example, would refusing to drink really cause disdain and rejection by friends? Would saying no to sex mean the end of a cherished relationship? Talk about how daring to be different is hard but it can be the most mature and courageous thing to do.

3. Hold practice sessions. Rehearsing for difficult situations can build self-confidence. This can take the form of playing the role of a friend who offers your child a cigarette, drink, drugs, or a date, and who won't take no for an answer. Rehearse words and phrases they can use in such predicaments. An emphatic "No, thanks." "I don't want to do that." "I don't need that stuff in my life." "I don't need to be like everyone else." "You're my best friend but I can't do that."

4. Promote self-respect. Ask his opinion. Treat with importance what he thinks, says and does. Self-esteem – what we call 'backbone' – can help a young kid to risk being different from peers and to say "no" when it counts.

5. Encourage participation in sports, scouts, guides and hobbies. These activities combat boredom, and introduce them to new friends with similar values. Youngsters who

have interests, talents and hobbies develop a sense of personal importance, a feeling that they are in control, and so
are less likely to be pushed around by their peers.

6. Intervene when your child's assertiveness wavers or
breaks down. For example if your daughter, under pressure
says "yes" to repeated invitations to an unsupervised party
late in the evening. It's your job to step in and say no. Share
your concern. Explain it's because you love her and care
about what might happen. It's always better to express concern over behaviour than getting into a power struggle.

In many instances a crisis can be avoided by intervening
early and making your child feel appreciated and loved. It
isn't easy, especially with young teenagers. But saying, "I'll
always love you, no matter what", can mean more to your
child and increase his/her capacity to overcome peer pressure, more than you can ever know.

2 Teenagers: Be Yourself –
Not Someone Else

"Why did I do it?" he asked. "Because I was stupid. My friends said, 'Here, try it.' and I didn't have the guts to say no. No one made me do it. I did it because I was stupid."

It's a true story. Word for word. It's a pity you have to believe it.

Every teenager will be tested in one way or another. there are no exceptions. It's part of growing up. Those who pass the test grow up. Those who fail grow old.

TAKING A STAND

Take Robbie for example. He was being pressurised to party all night. At some point he said: "Look guys, I have a mind of my own. I know what I want. Get off my back." And he went home to meet the curfew set by his parents, not feeling very good about it psychologically, but knowing at some deeper level that his manhood was still in one piece.

ADOLESCENCE

Adolescence is a hugely testing time. And yet, the ability to take pressure, handle it, stand alone if need be rather than follow the crowd, is one of the classic signs of maturity. The 'macho man', on the other hand is still trying to prove himself, still trying to impress others, still going to great lengths to get his own way. With 'macho man' as a friend who needs enemies?

Of course, it's very difficult to have the courage of your convictions and swim against the tide of public opinion. Of course, it is easy to be intimidated by one's peers. I know this sounds pretty basic, but it needs to be said: we have the right to say "no". There comes a moment when we have to decide how far we are prepared to go without compromising our integrity. We have to keep integrity intact because, somehow, it's all we have. Lose integrity and we lose part of our inner self. And that leaves us pretty destitute.

POSITIVE

Peer pressure gets a lot of bad press nowadays. A lot of people talk about it and say how destructive it can be. Of course, that is true, but it's not the whole truth.

Peer pressure can be a very good thing too. We can use the power and influence over others positively and constructively. We can make it easier, not harder, for friends and acquaintances to be the same person inside as well as outside. Happily, we all know people in whose company we have the space and freedom to be the best possible 'me'.

FRIENDS

If, however, we choose friends who are trouble-makers, rebels without a cause, the chances are that they will influence us into a lifestyle that militates against our best interests and may possibly wreck our future plans. If, on the other hand, we have friends who respect our values, our sense of decency and honour, we are unlikely to land in trouble or create problems for others. We develop and mature. We do not wither and die. A wise man expressed this important truth in a memorable way: Words may melt us, and deeds inflame us, but persons influence us.

So, the friends I choose maybe a deciding factor in shaping the type of person I turn out to be. Likewise, I can be the reason why my friend has retained that inner part of self that gives dignity, hope, and self-esteem. Or I can cost him his dreams, and indeed his very future. So much rides on the choice of friends. It's not for nothing that we say: "Show me your friends and I'll tell what you are".

OPPORTUNITY KNOCKS

We are, unquestionably, living in an age when choices, responsibilities and pressures come earlier than ever before.

Many kids are looking for self-esteem and love in the wrong places. It's not easy being a teenager today. Indeed, it's with this thought in mind I want to say something I have never put into words before.

YOUR LIFE

I doubt that I can do so properly, but I would like to try. "You are at a moment in life when you have to make some really serious decisions about who you are and what you are going to be. You must not let others decide for you. You must not let others treat you as if you are incapable of making up your own mind. No one can live your life for you and no one must try. To be alive is a dangerous thing. To be free is full of risks. But it is a glorious opportunity."

It would be easy for me to give you fine words and send you away with an optimistic picture of the future. But it would be wrong. I cannot paint a rosé champagne picture of the future. But I can say that your future and the lives of others, some of whom are yet to be born, depend on the type of person you choose to be.

DECISIONS

There is such a thing as asking for too much advice. Yes, by all means get advice. Professional people do not hesitate to consult experts. By all means listen to your parents and friends. Get the benefit of their wisdom and experience but in the end reserve the right to make your own decisions. Then, with all the inner strength and gentleness at your command, demand respect for your decision.

Something else I want to say and I am really struggling now to find the right words. People, lots of people I hope, love you. But I ask, who really knows you? Nobody! Parents, family, friends, teachers, priest? – they have a piece of the picture that is you. It is often true enough, but it's only a piece. You alone have the full view. That view will come to you when you are alone, perhaps, or when you lie awake at night. Sometimes it comes suddenly. It may be on hearing some words like "I love you". Or when someone shouts, "Get out of my sight, Stupid", or makes some other insulting remark.

A DIFFERENT DRUMMER

If you give any thought at all to that full picture of your-self (and it will come to you) you will know beyond all doubt what to do with your heart and life. It may not be what oth-ers would want you to do. It may not be a big deal in terms of money or so-called success. It may look like failure and waste to those outside you; but, inside, you will know you are right. And then you can look to the future with confi-dence and resonate to Thorea's stirring words: "If a man does not keep pace with his companions, perhaps it's because he hears a different drummer. Let him step to the music he hears, however measured or far away".

CHAPTER THREE

Drug Abuse

1. Saying No to Drugs

2. Will Power is not Enough

3. Key Players against Drugs

4. "My Kid is on Drugs"

1 *Saying No to Drugs*

Is your child taking drugs? God forbid! But without wishing to sound alarmist, the reality today is that you cannot prevent your children from being exposed to drugs any more than you can prevent them from getting influenza or catching the common cold.

If your kid hasn't tried drugs yet, that's great. Thank God! But even if you have a solid wall around your home forbidding drugs, that wall ceases to exist as soon as your child walks out the door.

As a parent, it may not matter if one, one thousand, or one million kids are addicted to drugs. All that matters is your child, and that he is not one of them.

COULDN'T HAPPEN TO ME!

Some parents think that this tragedy could never happen to their kid. Wrong! It happens all the time: to thousands of kids just like yours. They pray fervently, "Dear God, please don't let this happen to me. Please don't let this happen to my child". And while they pray, unnoticed by themselves, drugs are being pushed on their kids.

PUSHERS?

Most youngsters get into drugs because they are offered them not, mark you, by dealers, pushers or some sleazy character hanging out at some street corner or abandoned building, but by a friend. The "pusher" can be a "best" friend or the "nice" kid on the street or a "classmate" in school.

AFRAID TO BE DIFFERENT

I'm thinking of a young man I know, he took drugs for kicks and the drugs kicked the life out of him and kicked him into hospital. I asked him how it happened. He said: "I had a wonderful relationship with my parents and got on really well with my sisters and brother. I was doing well at school. I had a future to look forward to. But some of my closest friends started taking drugs and I was afraid to be different." He was learning the hard way that you either overcome your fears or they overcome you.

THE ROAD TOO FAR

Young people do not, as a rule, get into drugs or alcohol in order to assert independence and rebel against authority, but rather to gain acceptance. The 'get high', 'with-it' society, tells them it's 'cool', and so they feel constrained to experiment. They take a stroll down the drugs road, out of curiosity or peer pressure, and some go so far down that they never return. The journey back is beyond them.

The high risk, vulnerable years are between 12 and 20. Relatively few are introduced to drugs after the age of 20. So if kids can steer clear until then, they have, undoubtedly, an excellent chance of growing up into a drug free world.

NO PAIN, NO GAIN

Adolescence is that time of life when young people must grapple with the complex problems of growing up, become what they were meant to be and, thus, live the life they were born to live. The drug culture constitutes a major obstacle on the road to freedom and independence. Sadly, when they opt to take chemicals, the chemicals take them, sapping creativity, spontaneity, and vitality. Illegal drugs are not the means of finding yourself, as some contend, but are a complete distraction to that goal in life. What parents need to do is get their young children to experience clean and healthy living so that they can learn to cope with the legitimate pain of growing-up.

Much the same can be said about alcohol. More young people are drinking and they are getting younger – 13 and 14 year old children are now taking a drink. Sadly, it is inducing them into a lifestyle they may not be able to get out of.

TRUE TO ONE'S SELF

It is not enough to tell children to say no to drugs. More is needed to resist persuasive and seductive friends and acquaintances and be true to themselves and live life on their terms.

2 Will Power is not Enough

The simple words 'Say No to Drugs' are, of course, a striking slogan and a great beginning in teaching anti-drug awareness; but there is, alas, no guarantee in practice that it will be effective. The reason is not hard to understand or difficult to explain.

AFRAID TO BE DIFFERENT

When a youngster says no, the pusher does not give up. He usually responds "Why not?" or words to that effect. If it happens he's a friend, turning him down may be interpreted as a hostile act. Bill found this out the hard way, much to his cost. He said: "One of my best friends offered me an ecstasy tablet. I said 'No, thanks'. He got upset. Suddenly, it put years of friendship on the line. So I did give in. I just couldn't say no to a friend. I swallowed the tablet to please him". Important, indeed, as friends are, it is more important to remember that we won't have to live with friends, but we do have to live with ourselves.

HOW TO SAY NO

Simply telling an adolescent to say no is a good start, but it is not enough. You must, also, teach him how to say no and give reasons for wanting to say no. With a little coaching, his first brush with drugs does not have to be a moment of great drama or high-noon tension. He can be helped to meet the challenge and walk away with his head up.

His ability to say no can be developed in role playing situations. This can be done rather effectively in a home setting with family members participating. Portray the type of person who is likely to seduce your child. Stage a conflict situation. Script a dialogue that develops his capacity to stand

firm and not be rolled over. It could go something like this:
  "Come on, try it."
  "No way."
  "It's cool".
  "I'm not interested."
  "Not even a puff?"
  "Drugs bore me."
  "Scared?"
  "Why use crutches when I can walk."

If the pressure is overwhelming, have him exercise his freedom, play smart, and walk away. Applaud this course of action. Highlight this response as a sign of strength, not weakness. People who play with fire get burnt. Repeat role-playing scenes until he becomes self-assured and it's second nature to say no.

LEARNING FROM EXPERIENCE
If you know a drug addict in rehabilitation, invite him along. Get him to share his bad experiences: tell how drugs, for example, cost him the joys of growing up. Tell how he missed out on life; how life stood still and passed him by like a ship in the night.

There is, however, more to life than saying no. It's not enough to grow up anti-people. Anti-smoking, anti-drugs, anti-this and anti-that. We must be pro-people too, pro-life, pro-freedom, pro-family, pro-health, pro all that is good and fine and noble in life. More than anything, grow up seeing life as God's gift to us and the way we live as our gift to Him.

3 *Key Players against Drugs*

If you won't talk to your children about drugs they may get the message that drugs are alright. Talking, however, is only the beginning. You must go further and teach your child not simply about drugs but against drugs. You must give anti-drug education.

FIRST TEACHERS

Many parents leave drug education to the school, or simply leave it alone, because they don't feel competent enough to discuss the subject. Should something so critical and crucial as their child's well-being and development be entrusted to someone else, however good his qualifications may be? No one has greater influence over or interest in a child than his parents. Nobody! Parents, who take the time and make the effort to educate themselves on the dangers of drug abuse, are better positioned by nature and grace than anyone else to teach the children they love how to keep off drugs.

NEVER TOO SOON TO BEGIN

How early should this process begin? As soon as possible: Four or five years is not too soon. It may be difficult to accept the urgency of informing a four or five year old about drugs. You may protest at this suggestion: you may say: "What's the world coming to?" You look at your child. You see the innocence and it seems cruel to start preparing him to face the drug menace at at time when he is hardly out of diapers. Besides you may wonder how could little Robert possibly understand.

I'm afraid there is little room for second guessing here. If you question his ability to grasp basic concepts about drugs I suggest you visit the nearest pre-school and observe the learning process. You'll be amazed to find out what little toddlers

can understand. However, if your children are pre-teens or
teens it's never too late to begin.

If you have children of different age groups, I suggest,
working with them individually. Adapt your language to
their level of understanding. Don't use scare tactics or horror stories. Be well informed. The information you need
should be available in any good bookstore. Stick to the facts.
Because you are dealing with life and death issues, it's
always better to over explain than under explain.

TEACHING A FIVE YEAR OLD

For example, when a five year old is feeling unwell with
a headache and has to take an aspirin, use the opportunity to
say: "Martin, do you know what this tablet is?" He'll shake his
head "No." That is your chance to say: "This is an aspirin. We
take it when we're sick to make our bodies well . . .But only
when we're sick." Never say that we take aspirin 'to feel better'. The odds are he'll continue shaking his head and say
"No." So repeat what you said, adding, "We don't like taking
medicine or drugs but sometimes we have to".

Be careful not to overwhelm him with too much information. Young kids have a rather short concentration span. Boil
it down to essentials. Don't blind him with science!

TEACHING AN EIGHT YEAR OLD

Supposing Martin's eight year old sister, Elizabeth, asks
her dad, "What is cocaine?" he can answer: "It's a white pow-
der that comes from the coca plant. It was developed by medical scientists as a medicine to ease pain . . . but some people
began using it for fun because they thought it would make
their problems go away, and it only makes them worse".

TEACHING AN ELEVEN YEAR OLD

On the same subject he can explain the workings of the
body's nervous system to his 11 year old son Colin. He can
pinch him on his big toe and say: "The pain you feel isn't
really in your toe, it's in your brain. It travels along a net-
work of nerves which are like tiny wires connecting your
brain to the rest of your body." Excellent, if you can get your

hands on a school biology text book with an illustration of the human body and the central nervous system. As you explain you can point to the illustration and indicate what happens.

Continue, "Now, if I were to squeeze the big toe of a person on cocaine he wouldn't feel the pain so much because his brain never gets the message. The drug blocks it from travelling along the wire and into the brain." A parent's number one priority is to help shape his child's attitude to drugs, not necessarily turn him into a walking encyclopedia of knowledge.

So continue in this vain: "Some people use drugs to avoid pain. I don't mean physical pain but the pain you feel inside when you're feeling unhappy, bored or upset".

BODY NEVER LIES

Ask him if he remembers how awful it felt after being teased or rejected by friends or bullied by older boys or experiencing failure. Tell him "We can't always avoid feeling pain. Sometimes, in fact, it's even good, because the body never lies. Tummy aches, feeling of nausea, tell us that we are unwell. Pain may feel bad, but it is not necessarily a bad thing. . . "

"What is bad is that when people take a drug to get rid of their unhappiness, the drug wears off and the pain comes back. Only now it feels worse because the person has never tried to solve the problem. So he takes more of the drug. Eventually, he no longer knows how to feel good to smile or have fun without taking it.

If he uses cocaine enough times, it begins, to eat away at his body like mice eating cheese. The drug doesn't even make him feel better, but by then, he doesn't care any more. He can't stop using it. He can't live without it. He's addicted.

CRIME

Cocaine is very expensive. People steal money because they are so desperate and dependant on the drug. They steal from their own families. Burgle homes. Snatch handbags from women. Attack elderly people. Get caught by the police. End up in prison, sometimes for years, their lives in ruins.

Calmly make drugs a real, live issue. There is no need to be dramatic, moralise or preach.

Should your son one day have cocaine thrust upon him unexpectedly, hopefully, because of the way you have educated him a warning light will flash in his head and his instant reaction will be: this stuff is not for me. This stuff is bad. This stuff kills. Then you will have the satisfaction of knowing that you have done your bit in keeping the child you love off drugs.

4 *"My Kid is on Drugs"*

The solution to, as well as the prevention of, a drug problem starts with the parents.

If you discover that your child is experimenting with, or abusing drugs, you must not get stuck in your initial feelings of guilt, hurt, anger or helplessness. "Where did we go wrong?" Of course you make some mistakes, just like all parents, including those whose children never touch drugs. Rather than blaming each other or the child by saying, "How could you do this to us?" Take action that will help him now. Now means now. Start today. Tomorrow could be too late.

ACT NOW

If your child was bleeding to death, you wouldn't run off and take a course in First-Aid. You'd stop the bleeding. I'm going to tell you what not to do and how to avoid mistakes parents commonly make when confronted by this shocking reality. Solving the drug problem requires honesty and willingness. It's much easier to deny there is a problem. "He's smoking weed, no big thing." Ignoring the situation doesn't pay off. It takes time and commitment to solve a drug problem.

DENIAL

Perhaps Mary has been a good daughter or Brian a good son; even those from good families take drugs. The issue isn't whether a son is good or bad. It's that he is abusing himself with illicit drugs and needs help. Do not deny the obvious. Do not turn a blind eye because you are afraid you don't know what to do. Do not ignore the problem in the hope it will go away. Ignoring only perpetuates the crisis, and in the process wastes precious time. If the problem however, seems too big to handle, seek professional help. The wise man knows when to say, "I need help".

REACHABLE

If he is not out of control and can be helped at home the most difficult question we ask over and over is: "How do we begin to help someone to believe in tomorrow, believe that tomorrow can be different?" Human choice is the strongest principle of growth. Put simply, to provide options is to give hope that he can make it and be himself again.

CHOICES

The most important way we can show love is to help the one concerned focus on personal responsibility; to make choices. He on his part, must commit himself to stop using drugs. As long as he does his part we are on his side. We will not, however, condone, defend or support behaviour that is irresponsible. He is not to count on us if he chooses to self-destruct.

The solution to a drug problem is never simple or painless. If we think there is an easy and fast answer to addiction we are gravely mistaken. We must be realistic. We must not expect instant turn-arounds. The hardest and longest trip is the one back, there are no shortcuts.

BENDING OVER BACKWARDS

Do not make plea bargains. Do not say: "If you quit using drugs I'll increase your pocket money. I'll buy you a new outfit. I'll buy you a guitar. I'll send you to College and pay your tuition. I'll give you the use of the family car". Drug users look upon kindness as weakness.

GUILT TRIP

Do not make him feel more guilty. Do not say: "You're giving your mother or father a heart attack. Look at what you are doing to your family". You will only reinforce what he most probably believes, that you are more concerned about yourselves, your reputation, what the neighbours think, than about his well-being.

LIES

There is a basic guideline to keep in mind. You expect a heap of lies. Substance abusers are con artists who will say anything to get their next fix, and promise sun, moon and stars to get their own way, and get you off their backs. If you find substances in your son's room and confront him, expect lies. The standard one is, "That stuff is not mine. I'm holding it for a friend". Don't fall for it. In general the more serious the abuse, the more the resistance.

You see, the addict doesn't have the insight to reflect on his own experience. What happens is very simple. When you are desperate and have run out of options, then you do what needs to be done in order to sustain and nourish the drug habit. That means, if you have to lie and manipulate, you do that. If you have to steal, you do that. If you have to exploit the guilt most parents feel, you do that. If you have to, you imply, "if you paid more attention to me, if you really loved me I wouldn't be this way". It becomes increasingly difficult and then, quite impossible, for the addict to separate what he does, from who he is. He becomes what he does and he no longer cares.

When Hamlet, in Shakespeare's play admonished his mother, Queen Gertrude, for her immorality, she complained about his cruelty with bitter tears. Hamlet replied: "I am cruel, only to be kind". True love means doing our best for people in the situation that exists here and now, and in return demanding their full co-operation.

CHAPTER FOUR

Sexual Morality

1. Everybody's Not Doing It!

2. What Harm is There if we Love each Other?

3. Why Wait Until after Marriage

4. Love in Marriage

1 *Everybody's Not Doing It!*

"Why is it wrong to have sex before marriage?" "How far can we go, if we believe sex before marriage is wrong? Obviously, not the whole way, but when is far, too far?" These are some of the questions young people ask.

WRONG OR RIGHT

Engaged couples ask: "If two people really love each other and plan to get married, isn't it all right to have sex? Why wait until after marriage? Don't sex and love go together?" These are the kind of questions many sincere people ask. They are like the girl who wrote: "I am eighteen, I have been going with my boyfriend for over a year and we make love together. I've never really thought about it being right or wrong until just recently and it's causing me a lot of problems. On the one hand I've got friends who think it's perfectly acceptable. Then I've got the Church telling me it's wrong, and I really can't understand why it's wrong. Of course, I understand why it's wrong for some people, but my boyfriend and I have such a great relationship. It's very hard for my boyfriend suddenly to hear me say that we can no longer have that side of a relationship. Surely, there's room in the Christian faith to make one's own decision about such a personal and private matter."

PERMISSIVE SOCIETY

The media – tabloid newspapers, books, advertisements, movies, television, pop songs – support the view that "Everybody's doing it". Soap operas, T.V. soaps convey the same message: "sex is the norm." Couples are jumping in and out of bed and sex is equated with money, power and social status. A genuine relationship, if it is mentioned at all, seems to be of secondary importance. The result is that many impressionable young people are saying that being promiscuous is the norm. But is that true? Is it not the other way around? Is it not true that promiscuity is a social disease of immense proportions?

FALSE IMPRESSIONS

Sometimes things that seem so accepted and normal only appear that way because you hear so much about them. Have you noticed how even commercials use what is called the "bandwagon" effect? If people can be convinced that "everybody" is buying a product, a lot of otherwise clever and smart people will rush out and buy it – even if they don't need it or it's not worth the price. They have been taken for a ride and the manufacturers and sales-people are laughing all the way to the bank!

This is what seems to be happening with sex. The picture comes across that "everybody is doing it".

But not everybody is doing it. Not every teenager is having sex and many who are, don't want to, but just allow themselves to get talked into it because they are afraid they won't be accepted.

NOT THE SAME

Dating and getting to know people is a normal part of life. Dating, however, doesn't mean the same thing as having sex. Sex and love are closely related but they are not the same, and a large part of growing up is learning the difference.

"No" is a love word. Not only is it smart to say "no", it is enlightening. Is it easy? No! Is it worth it? Ask somebody who's been there and they will tell you that abstinence from sexual relationships before marriage is the best lifestyle physically, emotionally and spiritually.

The poet Robert Frost puts it beautifully when he says:

"Two roads diverged into a wood, and I –
   I took the less travelled road,
      and that has made all the difference."

2 What Harm is There if we Love each Other?

Consider this conversation from the movie 'Room at the Top.' "I do love you," she protests. "I would do anything for you". "Sure", he retorts: "You would do anything except the one thing any girl would do for the man she loves". So she gives in, the victim of emotional blackmail. Is that love? That's fear, fear of losing him, if she doesn't!

A man who says, "If you really love me, you would," should be answered, "If you really love me you wouldn't insist!"

But what if we want to have sex? What if we feel like doing it? What harm is there in it if we love each other?

FEELINGS NEITHER RIGHT NOR WRONG

Well, there are lots of things we want to do, aren't there? Lots of things we feel like doing? Does wanting to do something mean that it's right or the wise thing to do?

Our feelings never tell us how something really is. Our feelings can't tell if something is right or wrong. They only tell us how something feels.

Think of it this way. Have you ever travelled to some place and felt you were going the right way, only to end up in the wrong place and totally lost? The fact that you felt it was right didn't make it so.

PART OF BEING HUMAN

Feelings are a very important part of being human but they're not the only part or the biggest part.

To be really free, grown up, and mature, means to be responsible.

Before making important decisions – and decisions about sex are important – it's necessary to do three things:

1.   Understand the feelings you have.
2.   Think carefully about the feelings you have,
       the actions you can take and their consequences.
3.   Act responsibly.

What you do matters. If I fool around, I'll get pregnant. If I get onto drugs, I'll get hooked. If I don't study, I'll fail. If I play with fire, I'll get burned. Actions have consequences. Bad decisions can kill the dream and the future.

ENLIGHTENED WAY

Morality doesn't come from the Church. It comes from nature and ultimately from God. Ultimately, morality is not a matter of mere reason, 'what I think' or emotion, 'what I feel'. It's a matter of love. It's having eyes to see that God is the creator of the beauty and attractiveness I see in myself and others, and including Him in the relationship.

Sexual morality is not a spoil-sport. It is much more a way of helping people, men and women of flesh and blood to be their noblest selves.

3 Why Wait Until After Marriage?

If two people really love each other and plan to get married, isn't it all right for them to have sex? Why wait until after marriage?

Why wait? Unhappily, this has become a legitimate question. It prompts a further question. Are there things in life well worth waiting for? Think of two young lovers at the Airport saying goodbye and promising their undying love. He's on his way to Canada to pursue a university education. She's staying at home to complete her studies. Is he worth waiting for? Is she?

IDEAL SETTING

Is it not true that some things in life are so special that they require the best possible setting? Is sex not such a marvellous expression of human love that it demands the environment with the richest meaning? Surely, it is the you, you only, you always and no one else, relationship that provides sex with the best setting and deepest meaning.

The people who move in and out of bedrooms really don't know what they've missed. They may say to each other, "We're in love and someday we'll get married." But even if they marry they may discover later, to their dismay and consternation, that because of physical intimacy, they married without ever getting to know each other. Their relationship may never recover from the setback.

COMMUNICATION

Sex is communication. It's one way of sharing your sexuality and it always says something. It can say:
"I like you and I'd like to feel close to you."
"I'm not sure of myself but I need you."

"I'm not sure of you or me."
"I think I want to marry you – but I'm not sure."

Or it can say:
"I love you completely, I trust you and I choose to give myself to you for life. And now I want the whole world to know it."

The choice is ultimately between the lesser good over the greater, the superficial over the real, and the trivial over the tremendous!

BLUSHING

Charles Darwin, was once asked, after his discussions about how we are likened to the animals, whether there was still anything unique about being human. He answered, "Man is the only animal that blushes." He could easily have added, "Man is the only animal with good reason to blush."

In the bible, the first thing that happened to Adam and Eve, after they ate the forbidden fruit of good and evil, was that "their eyes were opened and they knew that they were naked". The animals in the garden were equally naked, but were not ashamed. They did not need to blush.

Biblically, to blush is to be self-conscious. It's to know the difference between good and evil. It's to have a conscience. It's to have a sense of morality. It's to be aware that you can fall short of God's standards and expectations.

EVERYTHING GOES?

A character in Dostoevsky's the Brothers Karamazov says, "If there is no God, everything is permitted."

A person who believes that everything goes, if he feel it is right, may feel free in rejecting absolute standards of good and bad. This freedom is the freedom of the sailor on the high seas without a compass. He is free to travel in any direction he chooses, but has no way of knowing in which direction the harbour lies. Should we envy him that kind of freedom?

A wise person said, "You can do what you like, but you won't like what you do." How true this is in the area of human relationship!

Part of being a loving person is caring enough to say no to things that are wrong. No is a very special kind of love. Sometimes it's very hard to say no. Sometimes it doesn't feel very good to say no. But we don't have to explain why. If we want to we can give reasons. We can say "No, it's wrong", or better "No, I love you too much for this". Saying no today makes saying yes tomorrow, in marriage, the beautiful and meaningful 'I love you' that it is meant to be.

HAPPILY EVER AFTER

Learning to be a loving person isn't always easy but it's always important. Indeed, learning to be a loving person is the most important thing we ever do.

This may be a little way off yet for the young who probably haven't even started thinking about it. But it's never too soon to become the sort of person who will live happily ever after.

4 *Love in Marriage*

As a matter of interest. . . just before I go any further, do you know any four letter words? I expect you do. Perhaps you even use them occasionally. I am going to use one now. I am giving you fair warning. But before you grab pen and paper and start writing to complain, perhaps you had better hear it. I'll spell it first: L O V E. And that word has much more meaning and is much more powerful than most four letter words.

A famous general once said, words are like battles. The right word is a battle won. An inaccurate one is a defeat. Today, the word love has suffered a major defeat. I can say, for example, I love chocolate cake, I love my dog, I love my family, I love God. From chocolate to God, all in one breath, it's a lot of work for one small word to do.

SACRIFICE

St. John tells us that God is love. Love is his very nature. "God so loved the world that he gave it his only Son." Giving is the keynote of loving. Not giving, in the accepted sense of parting with something we can do without. That costs nothing. But giving the very best that we have, namely, our very selves: no sacrifice being too much to make.

UNIQUE

Love, however, is one thing, but marrying is something entirely different. Indeed, we may fall in love many times before we find the right person. Love in marriage is unique.

A girl might say, "I like him very much and I enjoy his company, but I couldn't marry him, we'd be bad for each other". A man might say, "She's wonderfully reliable, fine to work with and good company. I'd miss her very much if she

70

left, but I couldn't live with her".

In words like these, people are saying that it is one thing to work and party with someone, but it is quite another to live with him/her because marriage involves a special kind of relationship.

A husband needs a wife as a woman to help him to become a man; a wife needs her husband as a man to help her to become a woman. He has to be man enough to make a woman of her; she has to be enough woman to make a man of him.

NO STRINGS ATTACHED

Love in marriage is giving the best of oneself, unconditionally and without reservation to the exclusion of everyone else.

However, and this might sound contradictory, but love alone in marriage is not quite enough. Marriage built on love is marriage built on sand! It is true that marriage springs from love, but it's stability should not depend on it.

FATAL ATTRACTION

Think of the Soap Operas! There is love and there is sex, but are there any permanent relationships? Why not? Is it because there are no real commitments? Is a relationship based on love and sex, without total commitment, therefore doomed to failure, confusion and heart-break?

In any good marriage, a couple will fall in and out of love hundreds of times. There are no perfect marriages because there are no perfect people. What is important, what matters in the end, is the knowledge that when we fail, we know we are still loved; we are sure of each other's forgiveness because we know, in our hearts we are totally committed.

BASE

Commitment is the foundation stone on which human relationships are built. If we are wrong about this we are, sadly, wrong about many important things in life.

Commitment is no accident, but an achievement of immense significance. It's the top rung of the ladder of human relationships. There is no way of climbing to that lofty height except by the demanding and difficult route of sacrifice and self discipline.

CHAPTER FIVE

A.I.D.S.

1.   A Life and Death Issue

2.   A.I.D.S. is a Death Sentence

3.   Innocent at Risk

4.   Wrecked Beauty

1 *A Life and Death Issue*

There are some very hard questions being asked these days. Questions like: What are we coming to? Where will it all end? It has to end somewhere.

There are many reasons for fear and anxiety: economic difficulties, recession, unemployment, crime, violence in our streets, drugs, alcoholic abuse and A.I.D.S. For these reasons and more besides, many of us are asking the questions with which we began: where will it all end? It has to end somewhere!

SERIOUS QUESTIONS

A.I.D.S . is a contemporary life and death issue, and raises serious moral, pastoral and educational questions. It is moreover one of the most serious health problems that has ever faced the human race. There is widespread ignorance about this terrible disease and many innocent people, especially young, are at risk. Sadly, many people are going to get A.I.D.S. and die in the prime of life. If we can stop the ignorance we can, hopefully, reduce the threat and spread of this killer disease.

We are, moreover, going to meet someone with A.I.D.S. or H.I.V. We are going to meet a family with someone who has A.I.D.S. How we respond to these people will test the quality and depth of our humanity and christianity.

PARENTS: FIRST TEACHERS

As a parent you may protest and say, "A.I.D.S. is not my problem. My children don't do drugs. They are not gay. A.I.D.S. is totally gross. I don't want to talk about it". But right now may be the best time to talk. Why? Because now is the time when teenagers are starting to make choices about

74

love and drugs - choices that will affect their lives.

Parents have a natural inclination to influence the development of their child's character. The underlying conviction here - a point I wish to make with some emphasis - is that parents first, and then teachers, are the key players in preventing A.I.D.S.

EDUCATION: GIFT

A son or daughter, like most teenagers, may be embarrassed, shy or unwilling to listen when parents bring up the subject of A.I.D.S. The fact that it is difficult is not, however, a good reason for silence. Besides, the young always know more than parents think! Education takes time, and it's one of the most valuable gifts parents will give their children.

Youngsters nowadays are tough. I see it everyday. They are not easily shocked. Parents should talk to their teenage children before they are faced with decisions about the future. They should not miss the opportunity to exercise influence on what is critical in their young lives.

FACTS AND FICTION

In this series of articles I want to present the best information so that the right choices can be made. I want to separate facts from fiction.

In any discussion on A.I.D.S. it is important to understand, at the outset, the difference between H.I.V. and A.I.D.S. itself.

H.I.V. stands for Human Immunodeficiency Virus. Human means human beings, not animals.

"Immuno" refers to the immune system, the organs and cells that fight off diseases and infection in our bodies.

"Deficiency" means a breakdown or lack of something; so Immunodeficiency means the immune system is damaged and cannot function properly to fight off effectively infections or diseases.

"Virus" is an extremely tiny germ that invades the body and causes the immune system to break down or collapse completely.

H.I.V. and A.I.D.S. are not the same thing. H.I.V. is the

virus that causes A.I.D.S.

The word A.I.D.S. stands for Acquired Immuno-deficiency syndrome. "Acquired" means you are not born with it. "Syndrome" means a combination of physical signs and symptoms. The virus may live in a human body for years before actual symptoms appear, but more about this in a later article.

WAR FRONT

It may be helpful to visualise the A.I.D.S. syndrome as war. The body is the battlefield. The H.I.V. virus is the arch-enemy. The virus invades the body with disease and attacks the white cells. The white cells are the body's first line of defence and like front-line soldiers are there to stand up to and fight the enemy.

In medical terms, the function of the white cells is to recognise infection and alert the immune system to begin producing anti-bodies to fight disease. Normally the white cells destroy these foreign invaders. But when the H.I.V. enters the body, it heads straight for the white cells and overpowers them. As the virus multiplies, it eventually destroys the body's natural defences. When this occurs the infected person becomes vulnerable to diseases that healthy people can usually ward off.

FULL BLOWN A.I.D.S.

The appearances of these diseases – there are two, one is a rare form of cancer called Kaposi Sarcoma, the other is a form of pneumonia called Pnuemo Cystis Carinii – makes possible the medical diagnosis of full blown A.I.D.S.

A.I.D.S. therefore, is a condition, not a disease. People do not die of A.I.D.S.; they die because the virus makes their bodies so weak that they cannot fight these diseases.

2 A.I.D.S. is a Death Sentence

"I didn't get H.I.V. because I was a bad person or someone deserved it. No one deserves to get A.I.D.S. I got it because I thought H.I.V. could never happen to someone like me. Obviously if I could turn the clock back, I would have acted differently, but I can't. For me the bell is tolling and it's breaking my heart." These are the soul destroying words of a young man, the father of three beautiful children, in the fourth stage of the H.I.V. virus.

PURPOSE

One of my goals is to communicate the message that the greatest danger comes from thinking I am not at risk. Teenagers and young adults are famous for their sense of immortality. They believe they can take risks and get away with it, that H.I.V. is something that only happens to other people. They are wrong. Studies show that even the well informed about A.I.D.S. have "it can't happen to me syndrome", that does not reflect reality.

REALITY

The hard facts are: A.I.D.S. is for life. A.I.D.S. is a killer. There is no second chance. There is no vaccine to prevent it. There is no vaccine to cure it. There is no cure on the horizon. Not even the most brash medical research scientist would suggest that there is hope of a vaccine being available before the end of the century.

ELUSIVE

The H.I.V. virus is extraordinarily complex. The virus mutates faster than any other infective agent, even faster than the flu virus, whose different strains produce an epidemic every few years. The virus that infects the Dublin drug addict may be different from the strain that infects the African addict, which in turn may be different from the virus that infects the American homosexual or the Asian heterosexual.

MOVING TARGET

Furthermore, when the virus actually gets inside the body, it rapidly multiplies and presents a constantly moving target for the body's immune defences. Even if it is possible to develop a vaccine against one strain of virus, there is no guarantee it will work against a second or third. Indeed, such are the individual peculiarities of the A.I.D.S. virus, that medical scientists are virtually unanimous in judging it to be, probably, the most formidable foe they have encountered.

NO RESPECTER OF PERSONS

The A.I.D.S. virus does not discriminate. It doesn't care who you are. It doesn't care if you are straight or gay, male or female, young or old.

BEHAVIOUR

A.I.D.S. is about getting sick and dying. Not from who you are but from what you do. That's the bottom line. A.I.D.S. can kill you, but you don't have to get it. You have to do something to get A.I.D.S. To avoid getting A.I.D.S. you have to do something too. You have to make some choices. You have to say no to certain kinds of behaviour.

RESPONSIBILITY

What you do matters. You have to make choices that will affect your life. So ultimately it is up to each of us. Ultimately, it is a question of personal responsibility. If we take responsibility we don't have to worry about anyone giving us A.I.D.S.

HOW IT HAPPENS

How do you become infected with H.I.V.? And how is the virus transmitted?

A.I.D.S. is not a sickness that comes out of nowhere. Most A.I.D.S. cases are linked to specific kinds of behaviour that involve sexual contact or needle exchange.

The A.I.D.S. Virus lives in blood or semen. To get A.I.D.S. there must be an exchange of bodily fluids with an infected person.

The majority of people struck down with this disease get it either as a result of having sexual intercourse with an infected person or sharing a dirty needle or syringes with someone who is infected.

When someone with H.I.V. shares a dirty needle to "shoot up", it is possible for a tiny drop of infected blood to remain inside the syringe. If you use the same syringe, you are actually injecting that person's blood into your bloodstream and you risk being infected.

BLOOD TRANSFUSIONS

You can get H.I.V. by getting a blood transfusion from someone who is infected. Before 1985 a number of people who got blood transfusions became infected with H.I.V. because they were given donated blood that was, unknowingly, infected with the virus. In the meantime, a screening test has been developed to detect H.I.V. anti-bodies. And since then all blood donated to blood transfusion banks is scientifically tested and screened for H.I.V.

PREGNANCY

A pregnant woman with H.I.V can pass the virus to her child before, during, and after birth. Sadly, some of these babies are born not only infected with H.I.V., but also addicted to the drugs their mothers are taking. Sadly, they eventually go on to develop full blown A.I.D.S.

HAPPY ESCAPE

The anti-bodies that show up in the initial test may, however, belong to the mother and not her infant. Unless the virus infects the foetus or infant, these anti-bodies from the mother will disappear within eighteen months. Happily these infants grow and develop into healthy human beings.

3 Innocent at Risk

A.I.D.S. is a disease that is fatal and spreading. It is an epidemic that has killed innocent people and, mostly, young people in the prime of life. In addition to illness, disability and death, A.I.D.S. has struck fear into the hearts of countless people – fear of the disease and fear of the unknown.

Fear can be a good thing – it's the beginning of wisdom but only the beginning – if it helps us to avoid behaviour that puts us in danger of A.I.D.S. On the other hand, unreasonable irrational fear can be as crippling as the disease itself.

Fear of A.I.D.S. is in the air. A.I.D.S. itself is not in the air.

NOT CONTAGIOUS

A.I.D.S. is an infectious, not contagious disease. You won't "catch" it like a cold or flue because the virus is a different type. Outside the bloodstream, it is so fragile it cannot live very long. It can only survive for ten or fifteen seconds at most. It is easily killed. Indeed it can be killed with ordinary soap and water.

It is important to understand clearly how the infection can be passed on and how it cannot be passed on. It is a known fact that the virus can only live at dangerous levels in blood, semen and vaginal fluids.

There are four proven ways in which the virus can be passed on:

- Sharing "dirty" needles/syringes
- Sexual contact involving the exchange of bodily fluids.
- A blood transfusion from an infected donor.
- A H.I.V. pregnant mother.

RISK FREE

You cannot "catch" the virus through everyday physical contact with the people around you in school, office, bar, supermarket, cinema, pub, church. Families living with a family member do not get A.I.D.S., even when they share towels, food, cups, spoons, plates and so on. There is no known case, for example, of a person having contracted H.I.V. as a result of fighting, or being spat upon. The medical opinion is that there is no risk of transmission because the infection is present in such small quantities.

COMMON SENSE

Nonetheless, I am not being paranoid or unduly fearful when I treat everyone I meet, friend and foe alike, as a potential carrier of the disease. I am just being careful. I am simply recognising its mysterious nature. I am being sensible when I put into practice the ordinary rules of hygiene and public health care.

If I have a bleeding finger I will not go to the assistance of someone having a nose bleed until I first attend to my open wound. Only when I have it cleaned and bandaged will I offer first aid to the bleeding nose. Ordinary common sense dictates that I avoid 'blood to blood' contact. This is a simple rule of hygiene and health care and no child is too young to learn this important lesson.

IMMUNE

As chaplain in Mountjoy I had daily contact with young men and women with H.I.V. and full blown A.I.D.S. If I had a bad dose of influenza I would not visit these prisoners until I had fully recovered. The reason is quite simple. One of the prisoners expressed it well when he said: "Father I have no immune system to protect me against infection. You have. I am more in danger from you than you are from me". He was absolutely right. I have an immune system to protect me against sickness. He, on the other hand, hasn't got one.

PREVENTABLE

A.I.D.S. is a preventable disease. The good news is that by

saying no to specific behaviour, already noted, the risk of getting A.I.D.S. is practically zero. Put simply: no matter what
you have heard, the A.I.D.S. virus is hard to get and easily
avoided.

SINGLE ACT

The bad news is that even one act of sexual intercourse
or needle sharing with an infected person is life threatening.
Put more startlingly: Each time you have unprotected sex it's
as if you are having sex with all his previous partners. Each
high risk act is Russian Roulette.

The implications are pretty horrendous. A person who
was sexually promiscuous in the past may have been infected in a previous relationship and may not know it. He may
be dating a girl who is clean. The relationship may blossom
into marriage. If it does, then an innocent woman is at risk
from a killer disease without knowing it.

So there may be some difficult questions to ask one's
fiance. Has he been sexually active? Has he experimented
with intravenous drugs? These are sensitive questions but if
you are in a serious relationship you have a personal responsibility to ask them. It's your life!

SIMPLY DON'T KNOW

Most people are not trying to spread A.I.D.S. Usually
they just don't know they are infected.

People infected with H.I.V. do not necessarily have
A.I.D.S. Often they are completely healthy. But once they
are infected they are infected for life.

A SLEEPING TIGER

The virus can live inside your body for as short as two
years or ten years, or longer before you show any symptoms.
During that time, you may look clean and feel healthy and
live a normal life, but all the time you have the potential to
infect others. Tragically, you can get the virus and pass it on
without you or the other person knowing it.

TEST

So you cannot tell whether someone has H.I.V. or A.I.D.S. by just looking at him – even if you are a doctor. The only way a person can know if he is a carrier is by having the H.I.V. anti-body test. (Sometimes called the A.I.D.S. test). Even if the test says you have H.I.V. anti-bodies, you do not necessarily have A.I.D.S. Only the doctor can tell whether you also have A.I.D.S., and only after he has given you a complete physical examination and carried out laboratory tests.

MORAL OBLIGATION

It is important to emphasis in this context that we have a moral obligation not to endanger other people's lives. If a person has a reason to believe that he may be a carrier of this deadly disease, he has a moral obligation to be tested for A.I.D.S. The reason is obvious enough, innocent people are being infected and some are going to get A.I.D.S. and die.

BLAMING GOD

People who should know better say that A.I.D.S. is something gay people bring upon themselves and get what is coming to them. Or that drug addicts have no one to blame but themselves. Or that sexually active people get what they deserve. A.I.D.S. is seen as a plague sent by God to punish these people.

Is God punishing gays with A.I.D.S.? This is the kind of question that has been asked for centuries. Each time some mysterious sickness strikes a nation or an individual community, there is a rush by some to see if God did it, and if so why.

If A.I.D.S. is, as some would have us believe, a plague sent by God on the gay community there are some real flaws in this theory. Gay women for example, are less likely to infect each other than gay men. Why, then is God punishing the men more than the women? And how do we explain this theory to the people of Zaire and Uganda, countries with the highest incidence of A.I.D.S. in the world, where the virus has been passed on, by and large, as a result of heterosexual activity?

GOD IS COMPASSION AND LOVE

When God is seen as a sadistic torturer, one who inflicts pain and suffering, our instinct is to run the other way and reject Him as callous and vindictive. In the bible, however, God is seen on the side of the sick, the oppressed, the lonely, the poor and the outcast. If you are gay or a drug addict with H.I.V. or A.I.D.S., the bible is not a book which condemns you. It is a book which reveals a God who loves you and stands with you. It's a message of hope. In his ministry Jesus never punished people with sickness. He cured them.

I think that the best of the Jewish and Christian traditions teaches us that the Divine identifies with the disadvantaged, the minority and the outcast. So how we respond to people with A.I.D.S. is a test of how truly Christian and human we are.

A.I.D.S. is not God's judgement on anyone. A.I.D.S. is not God's will. God is not vindictive. A.I.D.S. is not a sin. A.I.D.S. is a disease. No one, whoever he is or whatever his life style, deserves a fatal disease as a punishment.

DIGNITY

A.I.D.S. calls for compassion not shame, understanding not ignorance. It is important that we do not reject those known to have the virus, but care for them with dignity and kindness. Final judgement is up to God. Our part is to ease the suffering and find a cure.

When the question is asked, "Where are God's hands in this tragedy?" We must answer. "My hands are God's hands".

4 *Wrecked Beauty*

Each day in Mountjoy prison I saw the misery, self-destruction and corruption caused by drug abuse. Violence, contempt for health and life, A.I.D.S., despair and death itself are its deadly consequences.

WORST IS YET TO BE

I have attended too many funerals of men and women in the prime of life, sympathised with too many bereaved husbands, wives and parents, and seen too many orphaned children. I wish I could say I have seen the worst, but the signs are there for all to see that the fatal attraction of illicit drugs is spreading. I'm afraid an even more terrible crisis is unfolding and most at risk are the young and innocent.

IF ONLY

Hardly a day went by when I did not hear the sad refrain, "If only". If only I could turn back the clock to the time when I hadn't touched drugs when life was a laugh and I had my health and freedom and so much to live for. If only I could go back to those carefree days and start again, live the life I was born to live, and be the husband or wife or parent I was meant to be. If only! But at the impressionable age of 13 or 14 how could they foresee or appreciate the dangers of fooling around with drugs, the terrible price they would have to pay for their misadventure. But alas, as Shakespeare reminds us in Julius Caesar: "There is a tide in the affairs of men, which taken at the flood leads on to fortune. Omitted, all the voyage of their life is bound in shallows and in miseries".

"If only!" But if you are infected with the deadly A.I.D.S. virus it's too late for regrets. What is done is done. Whether the first experience of drugs was for "kicks" or out of curiosity or because of a stupid dare or the need to be accepted by the peer group, matters not now. A tragic mistake was made, followed by another and another, leading inexorably down the slippery road to addiction and slavery, and a life of desperation and destruction.

WASTE OF LIFE

The thing you have to remember is that many of the A.I.D.S. victims fell victim of the curse of illegal drugs at 13 or 14 years. It is heart-rending to think that this tragedy occurred at a time in life when they wanted nothing more than to be loved and cared for, and given the chance to grow up, get an education and live decent and respectable lives. Oscar Wilde was right when he said that youth is a marvellous thing, but wasted on the young.

SKID ROW

In the drug culture you don't care about getting A.I.D.S. or anything else. Your life has skidded out of control and crashed. You are on Skid Row and don't know it. Drugs have ruined the lives of so many beautiful people. It has cost them their innocence and youth, the joys and sorrows of parenthood.

Suzanne is, at the time of writing, a patient in a Dublin Hospital. She has full blown A.I.D.S. So, too, has her five year old daughter. It was with a cry from the heart that she said: "I don't want to die and I'm sick of being sick". She is twenty-six going on sixty!

ANOTHER YEAR?

She's a picture of wrecked beauty. You feel her pain when she says: "The worst thing about this illness is the uncertainty. Every year I say to myself, 'maybe I've got another year', and it surprises me long enough to say it again. I'm physically tough. I got that from my mother. It's better I face the fact that I am surviving but I'm not going to survive much longer. It would be extraordinary if I did. I ask God each day to let me live long enough to see my little girl make her first communion".

John is 29 years old. He too, is in hospital. He's in for a rest after a severe weight loss and a bout of double pneumonia. I know him well. He's warm. He has a great smile, rarely complains. They don't come any braver! He started on drugs at 14 years, just to be one of the boys. When he looks across the wasted years of his young life he has little memory of what life is like without drugs. "I'd get up in the morning and could think of nothing else but to rob and get enough money to feed my £80 a day habit. Nothing else mattered." John is dying, I hear his plaintive lament: "I'm going to the grave without knowing my own kids".

UNPOPULAR

I think I am well within the mark when I describe the men and women infected with H.I.V. amongst the least popular people in society. The vast majority of us have neither time nor feelings for them. They are perceived as different, less human, a public health threat, and better off segregated from our midst.

I have, however, experienced these people as exactly like us, every bit as human. They are good people. Some of the things they do are bad. What happened to them as they stood on the threshold of life, fresh-eyed and ruddy faced, alive with dreams and hopes, should never have been allowed. They never got the chances you and I got. I often ask myself if I had grown up in their back yard and been subjected to their temptations and hardships would I have survived and be where I am today? Honesty compels me to say this is a judgement call too close to make. I suspect, however, that I would have fallen a victim of the drug culture. In a world that is so hard and unsympathetic to addicts I, too, would be called a junkie, or something much worse!

CHAPTER SIX

Suicide

1. Suicide – Why?

2. A Tragedy Waiting to Happen

3. A Cry for Help

4. Causes of Suicide

5. Myths and Taboos

6. The Worst has Happened

7. Those Left Behind

8. Teenage Suicides

1 *Suicide – Why?*

"Life is difficult." So begins "The Road Less Travelled", by Scott Peck. So it is. No one escapes the pain. For some the pain is too much to bear, the lights go out, and they take their own lives.

Perhaps the most difficult task for me as prison chaplain is knocking on the door of an unsuspecting family and having to say: "I'm sorry, I have bad news. Your son died in his cell a few hours ago." Because a prison death is raw material for the next radio and television news cast, having to say too, with all the sensitivity at my command words to the effect: "I'm sorry. He took his own life. He hanged himself."

Suicide is a compelling and personal tragedy. It's a terrible bleak and lonesome way to end a human life. At its best suicide is an attempt, many would say, a failed attempt, to grapple with the basic riddle of human existence. Shakespeare posed the question as 'To be or not to be.'

FAMILY CONFUSED

Suicide leaves family and friends bewildered, confused and desperately searching for answers. "Why did she do it? If only I had been there during those last few hours and seconds?" You feel their pain, grief, desolation and outrage.

Though terribly painful too, we are somehow prepared for the deaths of elderly parents or close relatives with serious diseases. Terrible too, as are sudden or accidental deaths, death and dying is a natural part of life. We instinctively rally round the bereaved. Not so with suicide. Suicide hits below the belt. Society has taught even the kindest people to recoil when they hear the word suicide.

Most of us seldom give suicide a second thought. We have the illusion that this is something that happens to other people but not to me or mine. But when it happens and the victim is a neighbour or friend its impact is one of shock and dismay. If the victim is a young boy or girl it frightens all parents.

EMBARRASSED

Because of the stigma surrounding suicide we are ill at ease in the way we try to cope with it. We shy away from the bereaved. We're embarrassed. We don't know how to begin a conversation. We don't feel comfortable discussing something that has for so long been a taboo.

At a suicide funeral I attended a few months ago, the only reference the presiding priest made to the deceased was to say, "He had his good points". That's all. There was no word of comfort, no happy memory recalled, no story of the kind deeds he had done, or how much he would be missed by his loved ones. It wasn't that the priest was unsympathetic or indifferent but, rather, seemed more like a man who did not know what to say. And so he took refuge in the funeral rite and hid his personal thoughts and feelings behind prescribed prayers and scripture readings. The funeral service was surreal. The painful tragedy was neither acknowledged nor addressed. There was an awkwardness in the church and the grieving family knew it.

OUR TERRIBLE IGNORANCE

There is widespread ignorance about suicide. There are taboos and stigma that need to be dispelled. There are myths that need to be shattered. Until we are liberated from these constraints, the bereaved are left alone, feeling ashamed and misunderstood, bereft of the support and sympathy that is our gift to give. In the passing weeks and months and years, we refrain from mentioning the name of the dead one. We, mistakenly, assume that it might embarrass the family to be reminded of the tragedy, and we act as though it had not happened.

A loss, however, is a loss regardless of the circumstances. A few words acknowledging that sense of loss will be appreciated by the sorrowing family. A mass card at the time of the anniversary will be comforting.

IF ONLY?

Suicide carries tremendous guilt for family and close friends. One can grieve just as deeply for a friend as for a relative. It's not easy living with the painful question: "Why did she do this terrible thing?" or the dreadful haunting thoughts that he might still be with us if only we had paid more attention, or stayed at home that day, or showed more understanding, or the million other tormenting "ifs". Indeed just thinking about it makes the awful pain come back and it's as bad as the day it happened.

One mother, whose beautiful daughter committed suicide when asked, Why she did it, would say: "What I want to shout to everybody is that I don't know why. If I had seen it coming I would have moved heaven and earth to prevent it. My daughter was my life and soul. She was my pride and joy. I miss her terribly and cry each day for that girl of mine."

A PARTIAL EXPLANATION

While no one ultimately knows why a person takes his or her own life, suicide is not a bewildering mystery that cannot be understood. We can say something about it by way of an explanation, but only something. In the last resort we are left with a mystery just as we began with a mystery. I will attempt in these articles, however, to create a greater awareness of suicide and a context for making some sense of a death that seemed senseless and pointless. More than anything else, I want to honour the memory of these who left without saying good-bye and won't be coming home again.

2 *A Tragedy Waiting to Happen*

Suicide is not part of our awareness. Why then write a series of articles on such a depressing subject? The answer is simple. The rate of suicides has increased dramatically in the last 10-15 years and more people, very young people too, are killing themselves. You have read the stories in the newspapers. One of the stories may have been about someone you knew personally.

One of the problems with suicide is that we do not want to talk about a subject that has been taboo for so long. Some people believe that discussing anything dangerous will plant the wrong idea in someone showing signs of deep depression, and prompt him to act on it.

Talking about suicide does not cause people to be suicidal. Many depressed people have considered suicide as an option. Bringing the subject into the open, where it can be addressed, often provides a sense of relief and is one of the most helpful things we can do.

Besides if someone you know is hinting suicide then she is already thinking about it. You will not be giving ideas she hasn't had on her own. If she is not suicidal, she will reject the idea.

THREATS

There are, unfortunately, many myths about suicide which have little to do with real life. The most misleading one says that people who threaten suicide do not really mean it. This is incorrect. People who commit suicide often talk about ending their lives before they actually do it. But how do you know the cry for help is real? Many a person has threatened suicide over and over again until it becomes the story of the boy who cried "Wolf" too often, and for this reason is ignored.

DILEMMA

It is an awful paradox. Suicide goes against our natural instincts. Self-preservation is our most basic instinct. If someone really wants to die why would he tell someone who would try to prevent his death? The trouble with repeated suicidal threats is that they cast doubts on his real intentions. This may get in the way of our desire to help and may tip the balance dangerously towards suicide.

It is difficult to make sense of behaviour that appears theatrical or even mischievous. Hearing words like, "Leave me alone. I don't want your help." from someone crying out loudly for help, is, to say the least, bewildering for ordinary people.

This statement demonstrates vividly an ambivalence about being helped. This ambivalence is especially acute in the case of suicidal men. Approximately twice as many men as women kill themselves.

TAKING THREATS SERIOUSLY

Ignoring a person who talks about suicide is not the best solution. Every threat should be taken seriously. This saves lives. Just knowing that a person cares enough to take the threat seriously is significant to a potential suicide victim. There are instances however, when any intervention is useless. The person is hell-bent on ending his life.

Dismissing suicide threats with angry remarks like, "All right! Go ahead. Kill yourself, it's your life." in the belief that a get tough, no nonsense approach will snap him out of his depression or call his bluff, is not a wise move. I shudder to think of the consequences of such statements. It's a bit like playing Russian Roulette.

The two saddest and most common phrases heard by people dealing with suicides are, "I didn't think he would really do it." and "She just wasn't the type".

IN AN EMERGENCY

What you need to remember is that you are not the one who is feeling suicidal. To be a friend in this situation you need to set aside personal feelings and pay attention to what she is saying not to what you think her motives might be. It might be well to remember that anyone who tries to get attention by threatening to kill herself must be feeling pretty miserable. Something has gone wrong in her life. The best plan is to take the threats seriously and, if it is a problem you cannot solve, get help, call a doctor, tell her parents, inform her teachers, or telephone the Samaritans for guidance.

BE DIRECT

So if you hear someone say, "I wish I was dead", or words to that effect, do not take the remark lightly. Ask, "Are you thinking of hurting yourself?" or "Are you thinking of committing suicide"? Once the person in trouble begins to feel that someone really cares, the immediate crisis has passed. Your concern may be the difference between saving a precious human life . . . or losing it.

3 *A Cry for Help*

Suicide is not in our frame of reference. And yet, almost everyone knows someone who has either committed or attempted suicide. Indeed, many honest people will admit having considered, however briefly, the notion of it all. Suicide is, alas, no stranger to any race, religion, profession or age group. But when it happens, there will always be the unanswered questions: Why did they do it? Why did they not turn to family or friend?

LAST STRAW

You have heard the expression, 'The Straw that Breaks the Camel's back." Often, the things that build up to a suicide are like straws piling up on a camel's back. One straw on its own is too light for the camel to feel. A dozen straws are also too light to notice. But imagine a camel carrying a million straws on his back. At some point, one straw will be 'the last straw' and the camel breaks.

Usually people do not attempt suicide because of one bad experience. More often than not, the act of suicide follows several bad experiences.

INCOMPREHENSIBLE

A young man tried to kill himself after his team lost a key football match. Well, that is how it seemed to onlookers. People shook their heads in dismay and wondered why this otherwise normal young man would try to destroy his life over a stupid game of football. They could understand his disappointment, but wanting to kill himself was beyond their comprehension.

Actually the young man did not want to die over losing the game. He tried to kill himself because in a short period of time, his father and grandmother whom he loved dearly had both died. When he lost the game of football too, that was the loss he could not bear. That was the 'straw' that broke and nearly killed him.

Not surprisingly when a suicide happens we are caught off guard. The 'why' leaves the bereaved in turmoil. Rarely, is a relative or close friend able to pinpoint why he killed himself. Even when suicide notes are left behind, they seldom touch the real cause and are usually garbled. Sadly, the knowledge of the fatal flaw goes with them to the grave.

SUICIDE NOTE

Some people, may commit suicide on impulse, out of anger and revenge. And if someone leaves a suicide note, acting out of revenge, the effect can be devastating on those to whom it was addressed. In his book, 'Voices of Death', Edwin Shneidren has this to say: "In order to commit suicide, one cannot write a meaningful note; if one could write a meaningful note, one would not have to commit suicide . . . Life is like a long letter and the suicide note is merely a postscript to it, and cannot, by itself, be expected to carry the burden of substituting for the real document."

A TEMPORARY PROBLEM

Experts in the study of suicide suggest that most people commit suicide, not because they want to die, but because they have problems they think will never end. A far better question to ask is not, why they did it, but, what problem were they facing that seemed too big or too awful to solve? People who commit suicide are often torn between wanting to live and wanting to die. They see no light at the end of the tunnel. In the last fateful hours everything is seen with tunnel vision. Suicide seems to be the only way out. Given an extra hour the unhappy person might have solved the problem or met someone and talked things over. Tragically, a completed suicide (I refuse to use 'successful' suicide) is a permanent solution to a temporary problem.

STATE OF MIND

Most young people attempt suicide in their own homes, between mid-afternoon and midnight. They try it in a place where they are likely to be found and at a time when people are likely to be around. They really want to stop the pain, not die.

But what about those who are not rescued? How can we be sure that they did not want to die? Of course, we can never be sure but we can learn from suicide attempts that should have ended in death. We can learn from those who picked the place and means of death that left little chance of survival. A massive overdose, a bullet wound to the head, a jump from a bridge or cliff. When asked, "What flashed into your mind when faced with certainty of death?", most testified that in the seconds before they pulled the trigger or jumped off the cliff, they still wanted to live because, somehow, they knew their problems were not so big that they could not be solved.

What about the completed suicide? Some died because no one was around at the time to save them. They were victims of their own misjudgment and misadventure. Some died because they were so alone and felt that no one cared.

CRISIS WILL PASS

It is important for us to remember that for many people suicidal thoughts are temporary and that the crisis will pass. Prison chaplaincy has taught me that talking openly about suicide to a troubled or depressed person does not reinforce the desire to do it.

My experience is that they want to talk and want someone to listen. Afterwards when the storm has passed they are grateful that you listened non-judgementally.

CONFIDENTIALITY

But what do you do if a friend confides his plan to kill himself? That can be very frightening! Are we bound by such confidentiality?

I know one young man who told me that his best friend was planning to kill himself and had sworn him to secrecy.

The friend, rather than break the confidence, told no one. The young man duly cut his wrists, was rushed to hospital, and survived the ordeal. Can you imagine how the friend would have felt if he had died?

The right to life takes precedence over such acts of confidence. It is important, especially for young people, to realise that, when a suicidal friend says not to tell anyone, they are not bound by the secret if they feel their friend's life is in danger. They should tell an adult whom they trust.

When someone talks about wanting to take his life, do not be afraid to discuss it openly. Do not make moral judgements, or act shocked, or avoid the subject. Ask specific questions: "Are you considering suicide? Have you got a plan? Will you talk with someone who can help?" Avoid giving advice, and leave therapy to a professional. Your friendship and actions could save a precious life.

4 Causes of Suicide

Only loved ones left behind to mourn the suicide know what the pain is like. It is ten years ago since he took his life and his mother is still grieving. "Its too much to grasp. You really want to know what happened but you know you never will. He had so much promise, so kind but, at times, also so miserable."

Not only are the bereaved family left with a plethora of unanswered questions, but they must face the ignorance of friends and neighbours who believe much of the mythology surrounding death by suicide.

Few of us are aware, for example, that medical scientists believe that a high percentage of suicides are caused by undiagnosed manic-depression, schizophrenia or severe depression.

TRYING TO UNDERSTAND

Paula's story is familiar enough because it is true. "She refused to go to school. She was a defiant, rebellious teenager. Her parents tried punishment, bribes, incentives and counselling sessions but nothing worked. She was doing everything she could to spite them. She was out of control most of the time.

She left school at seventeen. She got several part-time jobs but either quit or was fired. "We were fortunate", said her mother, "that she was never promiscuous, or on drugs, or in trouble with the law. She left home at nineteen and tried to make it on her own. After she moved out, her relationship with the family improved dramatically. She held down a job as a sales clerk in a boutique. She was keeping in touch regularly on the telephone and seemed happy with herself. But she was sick and we did not know it."

MIDNIGHT PHONE CALLS

"After she died, we remembered the phone calls in the middle of the night. There were long silences on her part and then she would hang up. She was reaching out to say something but could not say it. Looking back, I doubt if she knew what she wanted to say. One gets awfully wise after a suicide and lots of things become clear which at the time went unnoticed. In between her mood swings, I began to appreciate what a beautiful person she really was, and felt a mother's pride and joy as I saw bits and pieces of myself reflected in her. I remember the years we fought. I was trying to instill my beliefs, values, ideas, good taste and style, and I can see now that she had heard me. But she had a serious brain disease and neither of us knew it. True we talked about her mood swings, but I thought she was simply a victim of depression most of us experience – the kind one gets over or snaps out of after a while."

"The day she died she didn't go to work. She was too depressed. She talked briefly on the phone. Then she picked some flowers in the garden. After a cup of tea in the kitchen she went to her room, locked the door, and hanged herself"...

DEPRESSION

Most of us regard depression as normal. But that is not true. What is true is that everyone feels unhappy, blue, or miserable at some time or other. We suffer too from other forms of sadness that come from being human. Depression however is an illness. Quite a number of people who kill themselves have unrecognised and, therefore, untreated major depression. Having to live with them is like walking through a minefield and treading carefully to avoid setting them off. To the untrained eye, mood swings, fits of anger, are quirks of nature which depressed people could control if they wished. But that is an oversimplification. These behaviours are symptomatic of something more serious. Untreated, they can in time, destroy human relationships, marriages, school achievements and job careers.

CHEMICAL IMBALANCE

The human brain is an organ of the body just like the heart or lungs. The brain has chemicals in it that regulate how we think, feel and behave. Quite simply when the chemicals get out of balance a person may suffer major depression, anxiety diseases or schizophrenia. These are the brain diseases which can result in suicides. Manic depression is an illness which causes extreme mood swings between great happiness and deep depression. Schizophrenia is an illness which causes a person to hear or see things others do not hear or see, and to behave in bizarre ways. Medical scientists tell us that manic depression and schizophrenia are related to chemical and physical imbalances in the brain.

Seratonin, a chemical in the brain, is also being studied for its possible effect on suicide. Scientists studying seratonin have found lower than normal levels of this brain chemical in people who have attempted suicide. They regard people without enough seratonin as a danger to themselves.

MOOD SWINGS

People suffering from manic depression, schizophrenia or low levels of seratonin may be deeply depressed or angry most of the time, not because their lives are miserable, but because the lack of chemicals in their brain makes them feel miserable or angry.

Some may receive good medical and psychological treatment but still kill themselves, just as cancer patients, even with the best of treatment, die. Some of those who are never treated for major depression may kill themselves, because they too are no longer able to live with their dramatic mood swings and uncontrollable behaviours. Sadly their loved ones may never have known how sick they were when they died.

IRRATIONAL

This is how one woman describes her pain of loss: "My husband's death was not the result of a fight we had. Suicide doesn't happen like that. People who are suicidal are often suicidal for a long time. I need people to understand that I wasn't the reason why he killed himself. We had a good marriage, and our relationship had nothing to do with his taking his own life. My husband suffered from a chemical imbalance that was diagnosed five years after we were married. I don't believe my husband was rational at the time he killed himself."

Suicide is a tragedy of immense human proportions. The bereaved need understanding not rash judgements. They are worthy of our kindliest thoughts and gentlest feelings.

5 *Myths and Taboos*

People say you will never know why someone you love committed suicide. The "why" you will never know is the haunting question. What was going on through his/her mind when they decided the time is now? Were they thinking of us? Were they mad with us? Why did they not tell us how bad things were?

There are many myths about suicide. What may be the biggest one of all is that someone, other than the victim, is responsible for the death. A man I know blames himself for the death of his son. His daughter phoned him from her home in New York City on the first anniversary. "Dad," she said, "it wasn't your fault." There was a long pause, and then in a grief stricken voice he answered: "And how do you know that it wasn't my fault?"

LIFE FULL OF PROMISE

His son's death fits no pattern. He had just graduated from University. He had good job prospects. He was a talented athlete and, outwardly, had everything going for him. He killed himself, leaving behind family and friends in a no man's land, with many questions and no answers.

His sister still feels the need to defend her brother, father and family. "My brother wasn't crazy. He wasn't on drugs. He wasn't a failure. We're a good family. And I miss him terribly." Her words echo poignantly the utter dismay a suicide causes. It seldom makes sense. Some people live lives filled with horror yet they keep going on. Others, seemingly, have wonderful lives and end it all in suicide.

BLAME

Parents, understandably, feel more guilt when their child takes his/her life. They can, at any time, review their life's history and, in a fleeting second, see what should have been done differently, and what might have been.

Like every mourner, they have to face the irrevocability of the loss. But they have the added burden of bearing the blame of people who say they contributed to the suicide by being an 'absent' father or a 'smothering' mother, or too 'busy' or too 'pushy' or too 'career-orientated', and so ignored their child's cry for help.

There is a widespread belief that if the victim has been loved enough and listened to enough, the suicide could have and should have been prevented. This is often the theme in movies and plays dealing with suicide. This is simply not true. Once the suicide occurs, it is solely the responsibility of the person who dies. This is a difficult concept to grasp because instinctively parents, family members and close friends feel responsible and blame themselves. The bottom line is that no one else is responsible except the persons who takes their lives, even if they are alcoholics, drug addicts, mentally ill, no matter how extreme the problem is. It is their behaviour, their choice, however limited it may have been. When everything they tried had not worked, when the pain was too much to bear, it was they who decided to end it all.

There is another widespread belief too, that you can cause someone else to commit suicide. You hear people saying: "You can push another over the edge". Neither is that true, unless that person wants to be pushed.

PARENTS

The deck of cards is stacked against the parents of the suicide child. 'Bad' parenting does not cause suicide anymore than 'good' parenting prevents it. If it were simply up to parenting, then all the children of 'bad' parents would kill themselves which is not the case, while the children of 'good' parents would not kill themselves, and this too, is not the case.

Parents blaming themselves is, perhaps, most potent when suicide occurs after a row with a son or daughter or after imposing a punishment. Parents would do well to remember the many times when harsh words were exchanged and punishments were given, yet their children did not harm themselves.

Husbands and wives, girlfriends, and boyfriends, are often quick to assume total responsibility, quick to say "It is my fault," when death follows the break-up of a relationship.

BROKEN ROMANCE

I noticed her, a young woman, in her early twenties, at the back of the church during the funeral Mass. She was quite distraught. I realised she was the girlfriend. She was carrying their baby but his family would have nothing to do with her. Two days before his tragic death he had received her letter breaking it off once again. I sympathised with her after Mass but she was inconsolable. His family was blaming her and she was blaming herself for his death. But I knew, and others knew too, that the cause of death was much more complicated than the letter she wrote. If the break-up of a relationship were the cause of suicide, I'm afraid there might be no one left here on earth.

HINDSIGHT

It is naturally, painful to look back. We see clues that seem obvious now with hindsight but, which, at the time, frightened us. She first talked about suicide and we pooh-poohed it. But of course if hindsight was foresight, none of us would make any mistakes.

Possibly we forget how really difficult it was living with her; the impossible demands, the tantrums, the mood-swings, or the outrageous behaviour. We forget the times we walked the extra mile or turned the other cheek. Then she killed herself and left us no defences. Now we alternate between anger and wonder. We ask again and again, "Why did she not give us another chance?"

Although it is easy to assume the role of victim, it is wiser to remember things as they were, rather than the way we so bitterly wish they were. Wiser too, to remember that we did the best we could with what we knew at the time.

It takes courage to let go of the victim bit, to pull our-selves out of the past and into the present and get on with life. It also takes courage to accept that we are not responsi-ble for the tragic and untimely death.

6 *The Worst has Happened*

The return to normal living after the awful tragedy of a suicide is, perhaps, one of life's longest and loneliest journeys. There are many reasons why this is so.

Suicide is itself a very emotive issue. Centuries of condemnation by church authorities have inevitably left their mark on public perception. We have tried to outlaw suicide by placing a taboo and stigma on both the people who killed themselves and their families.

The taboo prevented study and education by deciding that no one could talk about it, or learn about it. Thus the subject remained in the forbidden realm for hundreds of years. Consequently, until this century, little was known, and few felt sufficiently informed to express opinions on whether or not suicide is sad or bad, moral or immoral.

Discoveries in this century on how the brain works, and how it gets sick or damaged, have advanced scientific knowledge about mental illness and suicide. People are beginning to replace old beliefs and practices, now that there are medical and psychological answers and treatments.

STIGMA

Stigma on the other hand is the mark of shame and ridicule society has placed both on those who took their lives and their families. The stigma is the punishment for breaking the taboo.

SIN?

It used to be the case that suicide was almost automatically deemed a mortal sin. Those who grew up in the 40's remember, when victims of suicide were not allowed to be buried in consecrated ground.

WISER CHURCH

Denial of a Christian Burial was a formidable deterrent to anyone contemplating suicide rationally. Nowadays, this attitude is regarded as an unhealthy and misguided attempt at suicide prevention.

This is one area where the church has changed her attitude. Today, a more pastoral and compassionate approach prevails, not only for the sake of the deceased, but because we recognise that suicide is often the outcome of a disturbed mind, rather than a conscious repudiation of the sacredness of life.

GOD IS MERCIFUL

The average person who commits suicide has neither full control of his faculties nor the desire to die. He is not responsible and, therefore, not accountable for his actions. So before God there is no offence. It would be rash judgement on our part to say he has sinned, or gone to hell, or that suicide is God's will. Our individual state of mind is between ourselves and God and known only to Him alone. He is merciful even though He does not take away the sadness or mystery as to why someone we love would commit suicide.

NEW LEGISLATION

Here in Ireland, suicide is still written in the Statute Books as a crime. When a suicide is reported the Gardai are called in. A criminal investigation is set in motion. Personal possessions are impounded. It is a process that adds immeasurably and unimaginably to the anguish of an already grief stricken family. The time has come for enlightened politicians to frame new legislation in Dail Eireann decriminalising suicide. This would be an act of great humanity and would help eliminate a taboo and stigma that takes a heavy toll in damage to families where a suicide occurs.

INHIBITION

Unfortunately, we are influenced by the taboo, stigma and negative attitudes surrounding suicide. We do not, on the whole, handle it well. We are inhibited in the way we deal with family victims. We do not know what to say in its aftermath. Indeed it is not uncommon to feel so inadequate and uncomfortable that we say nothing for fear of saying the wrong thing or, worse, making the bereaved cry. So we shy away and act as if nothing happened. This in the circumstances is quite extraordinary, given the enormity of suicide.

LISTENING

When the worst has happened, it is, undoubtedly, true that we cannot imagine how awful a suicide death is. We can, however, come close to it by listening to the bereaved and becoming better informed.

CHURCH

Many survivors, for example, report that the Church is one of the great sources of comfort in dealing with a tragedy that has entered their lives. They speak movingly, for example of the funeral mass, the way it was celebrated, the meaningful scripture readings, the carefully chosen hymns, the sensitive homily, the solidarity of the local community, the mass cards, the tears, as life-giving events and memories, that sustained them in their darkest hours.

EMPATHY

Survivors know how hard it is for all of us too. This is how one family expressed their thoughts and feelings: "We dread people avoiding us or never calling her name, or behaving as if she never existed. We feel better when friends and neighbours come forward and acknowledge the death and say things like: 'We're sorry but we can't handle it either,' or 'I feel for you,' or 'I don't know what to say,' or 'How are you feeling' or 'You must miss her terribly,' or 'This must be the most painful thing you will ever go through.'"

The bereaved in their pain need to know there are concerned people who really care and want to help. Sometimes, however, they refuse to give the opportunity. The temptation to shut people out or keep them at a distance and suffer in silence and alone after a suicide, is real and strong.

It is a law of life that, it is in giving, we receive. One gets help in giving help. Friends and neighbours have to be taken care of and understood before they, in turn, can understand and take care of the bereaved.

As hard as it may seem, it is in the routine of life that suicide survivors get through days that seem agonizingly long, Suicide is not fair. The death of someone we love shakes our faith. Life will never be the same but it goes on. No one ever promised us a rose garden but throughout history people have suffered great tragedy, survived and been 'changed for the better', and have come back from a nightmare to live full normal and happy lives again.

7 Those Left Behind

There is a story about the mother talking to her son, John, and telling him he must go to school. He says: "But I don't want to go." She insists, "You must." He complains. "I don't want to go because the kids are picking on me." She says, "Never mind, you have to go to school." He protests. "I don't want to go because all the teachers are picking on me too." Then she says, "Never mind, John, you are the principal and you have to go to school."

THE MANY PAINS OF GRIEF

When sudden or untimely death strikes down a loved one, spouse, parent, child, sibling, the emotional pain can be so crippling that, at least for the time being, we don't have a reason for living. The feeling is: stop the world I want to get off. When the tragedy is suicide, it feels as if the bottom has fallen out of our world.

SHOCK

Grief caused by suicide is one of the most chaotic experiences we have to endure. The pain begins the moment the body is discovered. Our immediate reaction is either one of protest or denial. "Why?" "I don't believe it." "It can't be true." There is denial combined with shock. Denial enables us to break the bad news, call the family, plan the funeral arrangements, meet the people who come to sympathise and offer condolences. Shock is the physical reaction that makes us feel numb and dumb. The shock and denial are of a protective nature, enabling us to get through the life-ending rituals, pick up the pieces, and gradually get our lives together again.

"DON'T BE AFRAID OF THE DARK"

Life, however, will never be the same when someone we love has died in a ghastly way. The gap left in our lives is so large and deep that, for a while, all we can do is step around it. In these circumstances, it is normal to feel we will never be happy again; doubt our ability to relate with family and friends; wonder if we will recover from the upset. Months later we may be still in a daze, still going through the motions, with people saying we will never get over a suicide. But they are wrong. Survival is a basic instinct. It's what makes us human. Few of us have the 'luxury' of completely falling apart. We have jobs, children, spouses and friends. We have responsibilities to each of them. There is life after a suicide because we are the principal in our school of life.

Wisdom tells us that "nothing new has happened under the sun". There are no new things, just the same old things happening to new people. There have been suicides since men and women have inhabited the earth. People survived them and we will too. The future beckons to us and we have a healthy impulse to return because of that "Persistent breeze that blows towards us from the future".   (Albert Camus)

RECURRING NIGHTMARE

But first there is a long period of grief. A period of falling down, picking ourselves up again and again. There is , alas, no quick route back to life; the journey is uneven and unpredictable. We see her photograph or hear his favourite song or see her friends or his team play on 'Match of the Day', then suddenly, we are dumped, unceremoniously, into a raging river of grief, and wonder when will it ever end. At such times, it is only natural to feel we have lost all the progress we thought we had made. What we are in fact experiencing is legitimate pain.

"HOLD YOUR HEAD HIGH"

It may sound strange to say that we must work hard at happiness. What that means is that we should be good to ourselves. Going back to life means going to a movie, a football match, the theatre, a picnic, a wedding celebration, a holiday, and being able to enjoy the good things in life. Is it, I wonder, far fetched to suggest that these are the very activities our deceased ones would want us to engage in, instead of staying home and feeling sorry for them and ourselves?

It may be a bittersweet experience. The food may not taste as good, there may be lapses of concentration at the concert hall, the sky may not seem as blue and the sun may not appear to shine as warmly. Nonetheless, getting back into life means getting back into a routine that involves work, obligations and the things we enjoy. It means, also, recognising that we are not meant to live in glorious isolation. There are parents, children, spouses, friends we need and love and who, in turn love and need us. Life is God's gift to us and the way we live is our gift to Him.

LIVING IN THE PRESENT

The question is not, "Is it easy?" but, "Is it worth it?". One man told me he has the awful feeling that when he walksinto a room everyone is saying, "There's the father of the girl who committed suicide".

A mother felt she would never go back to the Bridge Club after the suicide of her teenage son. "How could I? They all know, I couldn't face them. But my sister talked me into it. When we got to the club, I had a panic attack. I barely made it through the door. I felt guilty being in a social setting, amidst laughter and chatter, silence and seriousness.

Afterwards, I said I'd never go back, but my sister persuaded me, and I persevered, and I'm glad, because Bridge helped me get back into the mainstream of life again."

Some people, sadly, cannot let go, because the deceased became an integral part of their sense of self. For them to let go would mean a loss of identity and disintegration of self.

LOVE IS FOR EVER

Remember John, the man who had to go back to school. Ultimately, we have choices after personal tragedy. Either we quit on life, or go back to it because we are the principal of our own life. Whether or not we realise it, we honour best the memory of our loved one by living life as fully as we can, and making up for the unfinished life he so sadly missed out on.

The garden of St Saviours, where I live, is something special. It has shrubs of all colours, shapes and sizes. On sunny days, it is breathtaking. In the midst of all this natural beauty stands an old sun dial. Inscribed on it is the wisdom of the ages:

"Hours fly, . .
Flowers Bloom and Die,
Old Ways, Old Days Pass,
Love Stays."

8   Teenage Suicides

I gave a talk recently to 140 Leaving Certificate students on prison, punishment and crime. I briefly touched on prison suicides. Once the topic was raised the students became completely engrossed and never allowed me to complete the presentation on prison.

Suicide was of great significance. They simply could not break away from questions which troubled them deeply. Afterwards I learned that all but a few had been touched in the past few years by the suicide either of a friend or neighbour or family member.

Why would anyone under the age of 20 want to end it all? It's almost beyond our comprehension that any young man or woman, standing on the threshold of life, would entertain such terrible bleak thoughts.

WHY WOULD HE DO SOMETHING LIKE THAT TO HIS FAMILY?
Sixteen year old Joey had been depressed after a poor school report at Christmas. He felt failure staring him in the face and dreaded the consequences. He could not see how things could get any worse. He thought of killing himself. "I'd rather die than be a failure."

Joey didn't keep these thoughts to himself. He told several friends he was going to "do himself in". Either they didn't believe him or didn't know what to do, because they did nothing. They had no way of knowing that his thoughts were more serious than the "I wish I were dead" kind we've all had when we are frustrated, embarrassed or lonely.

WHY?
Joanne, on the other hand, felt life wasn't worth living after the break-up with her boyfriend.

Joey didn't have to die. Neither did Joanne. If one of their friends had told their parents, or teacher, or trusted adult, what they were thinking, they probably would be alive today.

SHARING SUICIDAL THOUGHTS

Modern research shows that most young people share suicidal thoughts with friends. When asked in a survey "who would you tell if you were thinking of killing yourself?" almost 90 per cent said they would tell a friend first.

This raises an obvious question. If you are a teenager and your friend confides she is going to commit suicide, what would you do? Would you tell her parents? Would you bring her to some adult who might be able to help? Would you ask him about her sad feelings and plans to die or would you back-off and dismiss the threat as simply a bad mood?

TEENAGERS HELPING TEENAGERS

Teenagers, in fact, may be able to do a better job than adults in reaching out to troubled friends. This statement is not meant to diminish the important role parents and other adults can play in preventing suicide. It merely recognises the normal pattern of teenage behaviour and relationships.

Friends trust each other. They understand what it feels like to be a teenager. They find it easier to be themselves around friends, talk freely, share what they would never tell their parents.

They feel their parents do not understand the world they live in or the pressures with which they have to struggle. Maybe, parents do not listen. Maybe, they're preoccupied with their own problems. Sometimes it's hard for a teenager to believe parents were once young.

If teenagers have parents whom they can approach at any time, they are the first people to go to with suicidal thoughts or concerns about friends who may be considering suicide. But there are parents, like teenagers, who are uninformed about suicide, often fearful of the word, and who don't know what to do in the event of a son or daughter threatening to kill themselves.

REACHING OUT

Being friends puts us in a position to take positive and timely action to save life, and to be the first line of defence in the fight against teenage suicides. Young people should not have to kill themselves to solve their problems. I don't know any death which causes more sadness or guilt than suicide. I don't know any threat which is as effective in upsetting an entire household.

Not all suicides can be prevented, but if the life of one person can be saved by personal intervention, then it is only right that we learn whatever it takes to save life.

WHAT YOU NEED TO KNOW ABOUT SUICIDE

Suicide is the action of ending one's life. A suicide attempt, on the other hand, is a cry for help – a desperate effort to end the pain of problems that have become overwhelming. Learning about suicide can help us to answer that cry before it's too late.

In dealing with suicide and the suicidal there are many conceptions and misconceptions that must be addressed and clarified:

1. Most teenagers who attempt suicide really want to die.

This is not true. Most teenagers are very ambivalent and confused about dying. Where and when possible, we must try to provide the help that tips the scales towards life. Adolescents, especially those who are depressed, have difficulty believing they will survive adolescence. They often think their conflicts can never be solved, they see their problems as never ending, and their situation as hopeless. Teenagers, do not view death as a permanent situation, and suicide may appear as a temporary solution, the only way out of their pain and suffering. If only they were able to accept the wisdom of these words: "And this, too shall pass."

2. Nothing can be done to stop adolescents from killing themselves, once they've decided to commit suicide.

On the contrary, most want and can be stopped from taking their lives. Often a suicide crisis is brief, perhaps lasting only a few hours. If the adolescent is helped through the crisis he/she will be thankful to be alive.

3. Talking about suicide, with depressed teenagers, puts the idea into their heads and prompts them to kill themselves.

This is a widely held view. Actually, talking with teenagers directly about suicide is one of the most helpful unharmful things we can do. It shows that we are taking them seriously, by willingly discussing their darkest and most frightening feelings. They are, as a result, relieved to discuss what has so obsessed them, and are relieved too of a heavy and oppressive burden.

4. Suicide often occurs out of the blue and without any warning.

This is false. Research into teenage suicide shows that eighty per cent (80%) have given warnings or threats before attempting to kill themselves. This is why it is so important to be able to recognise the warning signs.

5. Adolescents who talk about suicide are just trying to get attention. They are not serious and should be ignored.

Again this is not true. Teenagers talking about killing themselves may be attention seeking, but such an act is a cry for help. Unless someone gives them some attention they might try something more drastic next time.

6. There is a certain type of adolescent who commits suicide, usually one from a poor family or one who is mentally ill.

People who commit suicide may feel hopeless and depressed but have not, necessarily lost touch with reality. Indeed, most people who kill themselves are too much in touch with reality – the reality of their desperate, never ending emotional pain. Their very thinking is distorted by pain. Hence, the unreliability of suicide notes. Suicide claims the lives of young people of all backgrounds, rich and poor, popular and unpopular, religious and non-religious, high I.Q's and low I.Q's, athletic and non-athletic.

7.   Adolescent boys are more likely to commit suicide than adolescent girls.

This is true. More girls than boys attempt suicide but more boys die than girls.

CODED MESSAGES

An adolescent who has difficulty communicating pain and distress offers "coded messages" that require a special awareness on our part to recognise and understand. As stress increases, he may be unable to cope and view his options as limited or even non-existent. A tunnel vision forms in which self destructive behaviour seems to be the only way out of his dilemma.

Suicides, however, usually do not happen without warning. If we can learn to recognise and decode the danger signs we may be instrumental in saving life.

A suicide clue may be:

1.   Verbal Threats. Statements such as, "You're better off without me.", or "I wish I were dead.", should always be taken seriously.

2.   Problems in school: A dramatic drop in grades, falling asleep in class, sudden emotional outbursts, behaviour that is strange or bizzare.

3.   Changes in behaviour: For example, normally active people become withdrawn and cautious, take unusual risks.

4.   Death Talk: A desire to end one's life may show up in art work, essays or ordinary conversation.

5.   Sudden Unexpected Happiness: A sudden 'high' after prolonged depression may mean he is greatly relieved because he has made a decision – a decision to commit suicide.

6.   Giving Away Possessions: Someone who has decided to commit suicide may give away personal belongings – music tapes, trophies, pieces of jewellery, articles of clothing and other prized possessions.

7.   Other Signs: these may include constant complaining, frequent accidents, attention seeking, prolonged grief after personal loss because of death or the break-up of a special relationship.

THE POWER TO PREVENT SUICIDE

It is possible that someone who shows suicidal tendencies may have no intention of ending his/her life. Don't however wait to find out:

1.   Talk Openly: It's the only way you can find out. If someone tells you he is going to kill himself, ask him how he is going to do it.
"Are you thinking of hurting yourself?" "Are you considering suicide?" "Do you have a plan?" "Will you talk to someone who can help?"

2.   Be a good listener: Listen with your eyes as well as your ears for non-verbal clues that show how the person is feeling. Avoid making moral judgements or acting shocked or disgusted. Don't argue or lecture.

3.   Show that you care: Reassure him that others care too.

4.   Don't sidestep or trivialise the issue. Avoid using "consoling expressions like: "It's not the end of the world." "You'll get over it." "Tomorrow is another day."

5.   Don't leave the person alone: Get help and, insofar as possible, wait until help arrives.

6.   Don't keep what you know in secret. If you believe a life is in danger, tell the family, or an adult you trust. The right to life takes precedence over a secret.

7. Don't feel responsible for saving the person. We cannot make choices for others. We cannot live their lives for them or keep them alive if they are determined to die. Maybe we can keep them alive long enough to get help, but we cannot control what he/she decides to do.

So while we may be able to help a friend choose life, it is important to emphasise that not only deaths can be prevented. To a degree, we are all responsible for what happens. "We are our brothers keeper." But that does not mean that we, personally, have to assume responsibility and guilt for a death that is unpredictable and unforeseen. In any situation in life there are things we can do and factors over which we have no control.

To think we have the power to determine what will happen in the future, or to imagine we can make things turn out our way, is an illusion. We cannot guarantee a happy outcome for someone we care for, however much we may desire it. It is, indeed, a mark of maturity to accept humbly our limitations.

CHAPTER SEVEN

Prison

1. A Hell-Hole

2. Prisoners are People Too!

3. Life Behind Bars

4. Is Revenge the Answer?

5. Verbal Violence

6. Prison Chaplain

7. Sea of Stress

8. Why More Prisons?

9. A Different Prison System

10. Dead Man Walking

11. Farewell Mountjoy

1   *A Hell-Hole*

You have seen the headlines, "criminals deserve harsher treatment". You have read the comments: "Our prisons are too soft." You have heard it said: £27,000 to keep a prisoner behind bars for a year. In these difficult times of unemployment, recession and dole queues, you think, and most of us are inclined to think, what we could do with an income like that. Then it becomes easy to believe that prisoners must live in luxury.

"I WANTED REVENGE"

You have heard the awful stories too. Stories like that of the young couple returning home late after an evening out. "As we turned into our road the first thing to hit us was that the car was gone. Next, we noticed that one of the upstairs lights was on. We stepped in and our worst fears were realised. We met chaos in every room. Things were strewn everywhere, the kettle, toaster, pots and pans. They pulled out all the books from the bookcase; all the clothes out of every cupboard and drawer. They had gone through all my private belongings. They took the television: the stereo too, my prized possession, a wedding present from my grandparents. I felt violated. I could understand stealing for monetary gain but it was the mess they'd made. If I could have caught hold of them, I would have done them damage. I wanted to go to their homes and smash everything. I don't care about their problems. I can't justify it but I want revenge".

LEVEL OF AWARENESS

I meet some of the people who do these terrible things and worse. I meet them in Mountjoy Prison as their Chaplain. I know them by name. I am not going to look you in the eye and defend the indefensible or excuse the inexcusable. I am not naive. I, too, have been the victim of crime, not once, but many times over. Awful as these injustices may be, I am conscious that one of my duties as Prison Chaplain is to raise the level of people's awareness to the reality of prison and to what it does to the imprisoned.

I have decided to write on the rather special kind of work we chaplains do, the place itself and more importantly, the people in prison; who they are, where they come from, what is likely to happen to them in prison and what is likely to happen to them following their release. The victims of crime, the criminal justice system, crime and punishment, our attitude to those in prison, whether or not prison works, alternatives to prison.

My task is not an easy one for the simple reason that crimes and the effects on innocent people are complex matters. This will require an extremely delicate balancing act on my part to get it right, between a sense of outrage against crime and a sense of dignity for the person who commits the crime, the rights of prisoners and those of law abiding citizens, mercy and retribution.

I AM IN PRISON BUT . . !

My task is further complicated by the fact that even though I am in prison every day, I don't know what it is like to be incarcerated. I don't eat prison food. I don't wear prison clothes. I have never been body searched. I don't know what it is to be a husband or father separated from wife and children. I don't know what its like to be locked up all night and have a chamber pot as a toilet. Nobody can look inside another person's body and feel their pain. But I can witness to what I see and hear; to the terrible effect imprisonment has and the damage it does to families, loved ones and innocent third parties.

Prison is a place of seizure. A prisoner is one who is seized. He is taken to a place of captivity. He is taken there against his will. He is taken there by force. The people with him are not there of their own choice. All are condemned to live together under the same roof.

A SEA OF STRESS

The prison environment is grey, cold, gloomy, harsh. It is depressing and depersonalising. It is a sea of stress. Everyone is in crisis. There are no creature comforts, no luxuries, no extras. There is popular belief that prisoners never had it so good, that prison is some kind of holiday camp. Nothing could be further from the truth. Even if each prisoner has a coloured television in his cell, a Persian carpet on the floor, and is served gourmet food three times a day, it is still a hell-hole, a place of squalor and degradation.

Brian Keenan, the former Beirut hostage, in his book "An Evil Cradling" describes one of his better places of captivity. "I entered the room. The guard stood behind me and whispered in my ear, 'look', I raised up my blindfold to find myself in a double cell. On the floor was a mattress with a brand-new light cotton bed-cover. On the stone shelf was soap, a red tooth-brush and to my surprise a bottle of Eau-de Cologne. The guard thought we should be delighted with our new larger accommodation. With the new bed-clothes and Eau-de-Cologne we were being treated like kings. But to us it meant nothing. If you put a diamond collar on a dog it is still a dog, made more ludicrous by the diamonds around its neck."

Brian's image describes well prison as I experience it daily.

PRISON DESTROYS . . !

Prison is a place where friendships are very shallow. You know it, but it makes no difference. It is a place where you can forget so many things, like the sound of a baby crying, the bark of a dog, the ring of a telephone. It is a place where you see and live with people you do not admire, and then you wonder if you are like them.

Prison is a place where you go to bed before you are tired, where you pull the blanket over your head to shut out the world. Where you try to escape by reading (if you are fortunate enough to know how).

It is a place where you find out that absence cannot make the heart grow fonder, where you forget what it is like to

have feelings for someone, where you forget how to love and
be loved.

Prison is a place where you lose the capacity for the sub-
lime. It is a place of pain and the people there are people
who have caused pain to themselves, their families and a lot
of innocent people, and regret it.

Oscar Wilde describes the sheer awfulness of prison in
his poem, *The Ballad of Reading Gaol.*

> " . . .The vilest deeds like prison weeds,
> Bloom well in prison air!
> It is only what is good in man
> That wastes and withers there:
> Pale anguish keeps the heavy gate
> and the warder is despair . . ."

Each day chaplains face the pain and suffering of those
who are locked up behind bars. The prisoner, however, is no
less a human being, no less a citizen of the State because he
is in prison. Ireland, being a signatory to the International
Convention on Civil and Political Rights, subscribes to the
principles upheld by article 10.1 which states: "All persons
deprived of their liberty shall be treated with humanity and
with respect for the inherent dignity of the human person".

2 *Prisoners are People Too!*

Society refers to those in prison as criminals. This is a terrible characterisation. It gives the impression that all prisoners are alike.

This is not true. There is, simply, no such person as a typical prisoner. Each person is unique.

PRISON POPULATION

The prison population is in fact a highly unbalanced social mix. There are no children. There are few old folk. It is either all men, or all women, but never mixed. It is made up of married, single, and separated people. People who are violent, dangerous, disruptive and manipulative: neurotics, psychotics, drug addicts, alcoholics, sex offenders. People who are passive, depressed suicidal. People who are immature, irresponsible, foolish, unmotivated. People who are highly intelligent, artistic and creative. The literate and illiterate. Young men and women infected with the A.I.D.S. virus. Those who are seriously damaged both mentally and physically. Many lack self-esteem and confidence, with none of the basic qualities necessary to form meaningful and dignified human relationships. Many, too, are more sinned against than sinning. All are lumped together under the same roof in the place we call prison. I suppose, we hope and pray that when released they will come back to us reformed, rehabilitated and cured. It is a lot to expect of prison!

DISADVANTAGED MINORITY

Interestingly, the most recent study of the prison population in Mountjoy prison, carried out some years ago, revealed that the people who end up in our prisons are overwhelmingly the poor and deprived, the losers in our society. In other words, if you happen to be one of the disadvantaged minority, the chances are that you may end up in prison. While we talk a lot about a just and fair society with equal opportunity, surely here is one area where many of us could usefully examine our consciences.

POVERTY AND PRISON

I am, emphatically, not saying that poverty makes people turn to crime. But poverty and deprivation provide the motive and incentive, because these people see themselves as the have-nots, second class citizens, and in a hopeless situation to effect change for the better in their lives.

Neither am I saying that there is more crime and less virtue among the poor. What I am saying is that recorded crime is concentrated largely in under-privileged working-class areas – not because crime may be greater in such areas – but because society's perception of what is a criminal accords with what happens in these areas.

WHITE COLLAR CRIME

Middle-class crimes (fraud, tax illegalities, motoring offences, company fiddles etc.) do not receive the same attention from the Gardai as do attacks on property. One could expand this list of "middle-class" crimes. One thinks of inside dealings on the Stock Exchange, the sordid side of "take-over-bids", property speculation based on "inside information", or "Political contacts", manipulation of bankruptcy laws etc. Nobody can convince me that there is less violation of the ten commandments, less sinning, less evasion of law, among the wealthy. Yet it is, overwhelmingly, from the poorer areas that our prison population comes.

PRICE OF INJUSTICE

Political and public debate about crime in Ireland concentrates largely on issues such as severe law and order policies, tougher security, longer sentences, a more punitive regime in our prisons. When the Minister of Justice unveiled her comprehensive thirteen point law and order package on Tuesday

14th December 1993, she showed scant attention to policies which might identify the causes of crime and try to tackle these at their roots. She showed too much concern with punishment and surveillance and too little with education, rehabilitation and reform of our prisoners. The price of justice can be great but the cost of injustice is even greater still.

If we abandon those who fall behind in the race, and continue to be concerned only with the survival of the fittest, it will lead ultimately to the destruction of all of us. Government must look at its social justice planning as well as criminal justice planning, and recognise that the two cannot be separated.

UNEMPLOYMENT AND CRIME

There are clear links between unemployment and crime. Many serious offences are being committed by people who are out of work. Unemployment is a dagger at the throat of a family struggling to make sense of their lives.

The unemployed become unemployable and are caught in a real "poverty-trap" from which they find it impossible to escape. Poverty and deprivation easily lead to alienation, and to young people feeling they have nothing to lose by taking the risk of committing crime.

POLITICS AND COMPASSION

Nobody excuses crime because of social conditions, but it is plain common sense that if young people are brought up in a culture of no job prospects, poor education, drug abuse and family instability, then they are less likely to grow up as individually responsible citizens. If crime is to be tackled at its roots we need greater commitment to the creation of real jobs and support for the disadvantaged. We need the politics of compassion and liberation, of setting the poor and the disadvantaged free.

3 Life Behind Bars

Picture the scene! After sentence a prisoner is taken from the court-room handcuffed, put in a security van and under police escort is driven to the place of incarceration. Once inside, he must surrender all personal belongings, watch, ring, clothing, in exchange for prison garb. He is duly photographed and fingerprinted. His personal history is written down and computerised for posterity. In Mountjoy, he is locked in a 8 x 6 cell with no running water, a chamberpot as a toilet, and in all probability, doubled up with a complete stranger.

TRAUMATIC CHANGE OF LIFE

The moment a man is committed to prison everything has changed including his lifestyle, reputation, social status, relationships and, most of all, himself.

By the time a medium or long term prisoner is released the world he knew will also have changed. Life will have passed him by, and the likelihood is that he will leave prison worse than when he came in. Families will have grown up and may have grown apart. Relationships, that once meant so much, may have deteriorated beyond repair.

Seldom, if ever, do we ask the question, "What do people become as a result of imprisonment? Are they going to be better or worse?" I can turn the question around and ask: "Are you going to be better for queuing up for meals four times a day, and eating all your meals alone (for a period of two, four, six years or whatever.)?"

NO RESPONSIBILITY

In prison, you lose the fundamental freedom to make plans for your life. Are you going to be a better human being by living in a highly regimented and structured regime where you don't have to make decisions for yourself? Where most decisions are made for you from the time you rise in the morning until it is time to be locked up in the evening? Where you are deprived to the extent that you don't have the option of switching on or off your cell light? Think about it! A man is put in prison because he acted irresponsibly in one way or another. He is placed in an environment where every movement is controlled, time is controlled, work and play is controlled, where personal responsibility is, effectively, taken away.

He is kept in this setting for a fixed period of time, let's say two years, locked up 16 hours a day. Then, on release, he is expected to take his place in the outside world as a responsible law-abiding citizen. Well, if that is our expectation, I think we are asking too much of prison, and those demanding tougher and longer prison sentences would, I believe, be well advised to think again.

PERSONALITY DESTROYED

The reality is that an ex-prisoner's chances of making it in life and finding a job are almost non-existent. The odds on his returning to prison, particularly if he is under twenty years, are very high. Prisons today are not in the business of rehabilitation. Security is what matters. Occupational therapy comes next. Containment is the order of the day. That is where the big money is spent.

'MODEL' PRISONER

Prison, apart from punishment, does little for the men and women doing time. If a prisoner obeys every rule and regulation, does not challenge the system or rock the boat or cause trouble, he is deemed a 'model' prisoner! Th authorities love 'model' prisoners! The fact that he may be conforming totally in order to survive, and becomes, as a result, institutionalised, a bit of a zombie and unable to function adequately as a human being, is of little consequence. The system, alas, is more important than the person. This needs to be strenuously opposed.

same time, there is an almost primitive cry for
The Criminal Justice Bill calling for longer and
rison sentences is in response to these feelings.
f we travel down this road, without reflecting on
quences, I'm afraid future generations will have to
e pieces in terms of human misery of both victims
ders alike.

ENEMY

he disputes that prison has an important role,
ss people respond to kindness and compassion not
r retribution, to love not to hate. The character in
strip expressed some wise words when he said:
e met the enemy and he is us." If it is revenge we
I have to say, we, perhaps, without realising it, are
y!

any people care for prisoners is not a priority. Our
es go entirely to the victims of crime and not to the
ors. This, of course, is perfectly understandable.
athies are with the victims. I can identify with their
outrage. I, too, know what it is to be a victim. Yet,
s, to be seen to respond to prisoners in a caring way
ably, interpreted as turning one's back on the vic-
rime. This is neither fair nor true. That the victim
pport and healing is not in question. Sadly, not
elp is given to the victim.

ENESS

the prison chaplain's lot to be labelled "soft" on
guess the labelling goes with the territory and is
ng we have to live with. I think of Gordon Wilson,
t Christian gentleman who could find it in his heart
ve, without reservation, the I.R.A. for killing his
daughter Marie in the Enniskillen Poppy Day mas-
1987. Was he in his mercy "soft" on crime? Or was
s forgiveness, saying there is a better way? Many
accused him of naivety when he made contact with

NO PRIVACY

In prison, there is no proper identity, no privacy, no variety. The last day of a sentence is the same as the first. There
is much boredom and psychological deterioration. Oscar
Wilde describes it well in his *Ballad of Reading Gaol*:

> "I know not whether laws be right,
> Or whether laws be wrong;
> All that we know who be in gaol
> Is that the wall is strong;
> And that each day is like a year,
> A year whose days are long".

All letters, coming in and going out, are read and
stamped 'censored'. Visits are supervised. Officially, you are
allowed one visit a week for thirty minutes. Multiply 30
minutes by 52 weeks and it come to the grand total of 26
hours a year. We preach about the sanctity of marriage.
How can you nourish and sustain a relationship with a wife
and children in an artificial setting, facing each other across
a counter table within hearing of other prisoners, visitors
and staff?

An extra visit called 'special' may be granted on request,
as a privilege, for 15 minutes.

SUFFERING FAMILIES

What is rarely appreciated is that families do time too,
every day of the sentence. Indeed, the great loyalty and
support given by many families never ceases to amaze me.
Some travel long distances, at great expense and inconvenience, often with small children, leaving behind pocket
money for cigarettes and tobacco which they can ill afford.
You'll never find these people calling prison a hotel or holiday camp. For them prison is a nightmare, a horror story, a
huge personal tragedy. A place they hate the living sight of!

GLOOM AND DOOM

Sometimes life in prison is too much. Some are not able
to cope. The lights go out. They give up. They die.

I will always remember John. He died in his cell. He

hanged himself. Because suicide is a crime on our statute books, the police took away his personal belongings for examination. Six weeks later they returned them to the chaplain's office. Among the bits and pieces was a book of poems compiled by Frank Delaney. It was called Silver Apples, Golden Apples: a title taken from the last two lines of Yeat's poem "The Song of Wandering Aengus".

> "The Silver Apples of the Moon
> The Golden Apples of the Sun".

I was curious to see the index of poems. I opened the book and to my surprise I saw scribbled on the inside of the cover John's goodbye to the lonely and awful world of prison:

> "Farewell, Farewell to my lonely cell,
> Farewell, Farewell for ever,
> For many is the lonely mile I have walked,
> From your window to your door,
> Farewell, Farewell forever".

RELEASE

Coming out of prison can be, equally, traumatic. A person should, on release, be treated as a full and equal member of society. Justice demands it. Rarely, is this the case. The reality is that for many prisoners, release leads to further punishment. They are stigmatised as criminals. They are discriminated against in the job market. All the talk about the prisoner paying his debt is lip service. Society, neither forgives nor forgets. Society rejects them when they are sent to prison and rejects them again when they are released.

There is a character in Greek mythology called Sisyhus. He was condemned by the Gods to roll a large stone up a mountain. When he reached the top he had to watch the stone roll down again. He pushed the huge stone up once more, and again it rolled back, and this went on unceasingly. Poor Sisyhus! Sadly, he captures for me the plight of so many of our prisoners, as they try to face life on the outside after release.

4 Is Revenge the A

The headlines scream at u
to shock. "Rapist strikes agai
beaten to death . .! Savage at
attacked with iron bar . . !" a
low. Find the culprit. Bring h
throw away the key. Castrate
island. Bring back the death
punishment.

I think these sentiments ar
temporary attitudes towards
think it is true to say that beh
discern, on the one hand, fear
other, a desire for revenge – an
a tooth. And yet if everyone
wrong-doing, I'm afraid we'd
Revenge is never the enlighten

AN EYE FOR AN EYE

People are scared. I can
anger that demands an eye for
ings of fear, horror and revulsio
minds and hearts particularly,
and sexual, towards the young
good if it motivates us to positiv
can't live on it. Because if we
become victims too. The abused

Society, of course, must be p
people. We have a basic right t
our homes; to walk the streets f
have the legitimate expectation t
dalised nor our hard earned belo

At th
revenge.
harsher
And yet,
the cons
pick up
and offe

MET TH
No
nonethe
revenge
the com
"We hav
seek, the
the enen

VICTIM
For
sympath
perpetra
My sym
sense of
nowada
is, inva
tims of
needs s
enough

FORGI
It's
crime.
someth
that gre
to forg
belove
sacre in
he, in
people

NO PRIVACY

In prison, there is no proper identity, no privacy, no variety. The last day of a sentence is the same as the first. There is much boredom and psychological deterioration. Oscar Wilde describes it well in his *Ballad of Reading Gaol:*

> "I know not whether laws be right,
> Or whether laws be wrong;
> All that we know who be in gaol
> Is that the wall is strong;
> And that each day is like a year,
> A year whose days are long".

All letters, coming in and going out, are read and stamped 'censored'. Visits are supervised. Officially, you are allowed one visit a week for thirty minutes. Multiply 30 minutes by 52 weeks and it come to the grand total of 26 hours a year. We preach about the sanctity of marriage. How can you nourish and sustain a relationship with a wife and children in an artificial setting, facing each other across a counter table within hearing of other prisoners, visitors and staff?

An extra visit called 'special' may be granted on request, as a privilege, for 15 minutes.

SUFFERING FAMILIES

What is rarely appreciated is that families do time too, every day of the sentence. Indeed, the great loyalty and support given by many families never ceases to amaze me. Some travel long distances, at great expense and inconvenience, often with small children, leaving behind pocket money for cigarettes and tobacco which they can ill afford. You'll never find these people calling prison a hotel or holiday camp. For them prison is a nightmare, a horror story, a huge personal tragedy. A place they hate the living sight of!

GLOOM AND DOOM

Sometimes life in prison is too much. Some are not able to cope. The lights go out. They give up. They die.

I will always remember John. He died in his cell. He

hanged himself. Because suicide is a crime on our statute books, the police took away his personal belongings for examination. Six weeks later they returned them to the chaplain's office. Among the bits and pieces was a book of poems compiled by Frank Delaney. It was called Silver Apples, Golden Apples: a title taken from the last two lines of Yeat's poem "The Song of Wandering Aengus".

>"The Silver Apples of the Moon
>The Golden Apples of the Sun".

I was curious to see the index of poems. I opened the book and to my surprise I saw scribbled on the inside of the cover John's goodbye to the lonely and awful world of prison:

>"Farewell, Farewell to my lonely cell,
>Farewell, Farewell for ever,
>For many is the lonely mile I have walked,
>From your window to your door,
>Farewell, Farewell forever".

RELEASE

Coming out of prison can be, equally, traumatic. A person should, on release, be treated as a full and equal member of society. Justice demands it. Rarely, is this the case. The reality is that for many prisoners, release leads to further punishment. They are stigmatised as criminals. They are discriminated against in the job market. All the talk about the prisoner paying his debt is lip service. Society, neither forgives nor forgets. Society rejects them when they are sent to prison and rejects them again when they are released.

There is a character in Greek mythology called Sisyhus. He was condemned by the Gods to roll a large stone up a mountain. When he reached the top he had to watch the stone roll down again. He pushed the huge stone up once more, and again it rolled back, and this went on unceasingly. Poor Sisyhus! Sadly, he captures for me the plight of so many of our prisoners, as they try to face life on the outside after release.

4 Is Revenge the Answer?

The headlines scream at us. They are losing their power to shock. "Rapist strikes again . . ! Elderly man living alone beaten to death . .! Savage attack on young girl . . ! Woman attacked with iron bar . . !" and so on. Angry reactions follow. Find the culprit. Bring him to justice. Lock him up and throw away the key. Castrate them. Banish them to a desert island. Bring back the death penalty. Bring back corporal punishment.

I think these sentiments are an accurate reflection of contemporary attitudes towards people who commit crime. I think it is true to say that behind these sentiments one can discern, on the one hand, fear for one's safety, and on the other, a desire for revenge – an eye for an eye and a tooth for a tooth. And yet if everyone insisted on this approach to wrong-doing, I'm afraid we'd be all blind and toothless! Revenge is never the enlightened way.

AN EYE FOR AN EYE

People are scared. I can understand completely the anger that demands an eye for an eye. I appreciate the feelings of fear, horror and revulsion that violent crime creates in minds and hearts particularly, crimes of violence, physical and sexual, towards the young and elderly. Anger can be good if it motivates us to positive action. But be warned. We can't live on it. Because if we live on anger and rage, we become victims too. The abused becomes the abuser.

Society, of course, must be protected against dangerous people. We have a basic right to live in peace and quiet in our homes; to walk the streets feeling safe and secure. We have the legitimate expectation that our property is not vandalised nor our hard earned belongings stolen.

At the same time, there is an almost primitive cry for revenge. The Criminal Justice Bill calling for longer and harsher prison sentences is in response to these feelings. And yet, if we travel down this road, without reflecting on the consequences, I'm afraid future generations will have to pick up the pieces in terms of human misery of both victims and offenders alike.

MET THE ENEMY

No one disputes that prison has an important role, nonetheless people respond to kindness and compassion not revenge or retribution, to love not to hate. The character in the comic strip expressed some wise words when he said: "We have met the enemy and he is us." If it is revenge we seek, then I have to say, we, perhaps, without realising it, are the enemy!

VICTIMS

For many people care for prisoners is not a priority. Our sympathies go entirely to the victims of crime and not to the perpetrators. This, of course, is perfectly understandable. My sympathies are with the victims. I can identify with their sense of outrage. I, too, know what it is to be a victim. Yet, nowadays, to be seen to respond to prisoners in a caring way is, invariably, interpreted as turning one's back on the victims of crime. This is neither fair nor true. That the victim needs support and healing is not in question. Sadly, not enough help is given to the victim.

FORGIVENESS

It's the prison chaplain's lot to be labelled "soft" on crime. I guess the labelling goes with the territory and is something we have to live with. I think of Gordon Wilson, that great Christian gentleman who could find it in his heart to forgive, without reservation, the I.R.A. for killing his beloved daughter Marie in the Enniskillen Poppy Day massacre in 1987. Was he in his mercy "soft" on crime? Or was he, in his forgiveness, saying there is a better way? Many people accused him of naivety when he made contact with the I.R.A. in a bid to end the campaign of violence in Northern Ireland. Asked what he would say to them, he said he would approach them as God's creatures." The I.R.A. is composed of human beings like ourselves, they have suffered too, just as we have. We all have the capacity for change." His peace initiative did not, as we know, bear fruit. "I do not believe the discussion with them has brought us any closer to peace, not an inch closer." he said. "I tried, I failed, my conscience is clear." Soft? No! Naive? Never! We need a vision to inspire us to look beyond what we are, to what we are capable of becoming. We need the truth that will set us free to be what we were meant to be.

HUMAN DIGNITY

Man is made in the image and likeness of God. He is – whether good or bad, educated or ignorant, useful or useless – a being with a unique dignity which nothing can take away from him.

In this vision, every man and woman, without exception, has been redeemed by Christ and is worthy of reverence and respect. Never is this reverence more needed than when man appears least God-like, for it is then he runs the greatest danger of being treated less than he is.

Being made in the image and likeness of God does not, however, exhaust the content of the christian image of man. Man is also weak. A human being capable of evil. Even when highly motivated and well-intentioned, we often make wrong judgements and decisions.

To speak of him as a sinner is not to demean him, still less to lose hope in him. In fact, it is part of the respect we owe man that, other things being equal, we presume he is responsible for what he does. "To be punished" wrote C. S. Lewis, "because we have deserved it . . . is to be treated as a human person made in God's image."

CIVILISED WAY

In an ideal world there would be no prisons. We would all love our neighbours as ourselves and I would be out of a job! No matter how much we wish it to be otherwise, we do not live in an ideal world. Whether we like it or not, prisons will be with us for the foreseeable future. What happens, however, in prisons is the responsibility of each of us.

No prisoner should suffer more than his or her share. A man is sent to prison as punishment, not for punishment. In a civilised society loss of liberty must be deemed punishment enough. A civilised society, will, moreover, find ways of not inflicting further punishment, for this, too, is a matter of justice.

"The mind and temper of the country, in regard to the treatment of crime and criminals, is one of the unfailing tests of the civilisation of any country." These words of Winston Churchill are as relevant and timely today as when first spoken in 1910.

5 *Verbal Violence*

After the two ten year old boys were found guilty of the murder of the three year old Liverpool toddler, James Bolger, in November 1993, a crowd of two hundred people gathered outside the Court. When the police vans drove the boys away, there were shouts "Kill them", "Hang them". A middle-aged woman, a mother herself, said they should be stoned to death. The father of two young boys said that if one of his sons committed such a crime, the case would never get to court, "I'd kill him. You think I wouldn't. Try me." The headline on a National newspaper screamed, "These two monsters could have been your children". Frequently, sub-editors in news items resort to inflammatory adjectives to describe individuals guilty of violent crimes as "hooligans", "scum", "terrorists" and the like. "Animal gets jail", is a typical headline.

A minister of Justice referred to the prisoners who rioted in Mountjoy Jail in September 1991 as "thugs". A young man was called "Junkie" in Court by a judge. He immediately protested: "Your honour, I'm not a junkie. I'm a man with a drug addiction problem". The judge apologised on the spot. A prisoner showed me a Swastika on his arm. "I never knew what it stood for when I was tattooed. Now I'm being called a Nazi. I'm no Nazi."

I expect most of us think of ourselves as peaceful, non-violent people. We are repulsed by acts of violence. But there are other ways, besides physical violence, of violating people. I remember, when I was young, we used to chant the ditty "sticks and stones will break my bones but names will never hurt me". But that is not true.

STICKS AND STONES

The psychological damage inflicted by name-calling can be more devastating and long term in its effects:

"Sticks and Stones may break my bones
But words can also hurt me:
Stones and Sticks break only skin
While words are ghosts that haunt me.

Slant and curved the word swords fall
To pierce and stick inside me:
Bats and bricks may ache through bones
But words can mortify me.

Pain from words has left its scar
On mind and heart that's tender:
Cuts and bruises now have healed
It's words that I remember."

OBSESSED WITH VIOLENCE

People who are quick to condemn acts of physical violence out of hand have, at times, a pretty narrow concept of what constitutes violence. They fail to see that calling people "animals" "monsters", "scumbags", "junkies" is verbal violence. It serves only to reinforce already existing biases and prejudices, as well as to develop negative attitudes in people who may be sympathetic and well-disposed.   I believe we have become obsessed with violence as the solution to violence. We need to see that violence breeds violence. Sadly when we victimise people they in turn victimise us.   The words of the poet Robert Burns are immortal: "Man's inhumanity to man makes countless thousands mourn."

By referring to people as "monsters", "beasts", we separate them from ourselves, as if they were not human beings. I understand how hard it is to claim them as "us", because we then have to claim the bad and the ugly in our own nature. As long as we can deny the negative in ourselves, we can remain outwardly superior, detached and self-righteous.

This is of course, far more comfortable, but, alas, untrue.

However, unpalatable, somewhere deep in all of us, is the capacity to project our pain and shame, in large and small ways, onto other people. We want no one to see us as we see ourselves. We hide behind all kinds of recriminations. We condemn in others what is inadequate in ourselves.

SEEING CHRIST

A Jekyll and Hyde exists in all of us without exception. In all of us, too, there is a Christ. If we find difficulty in acknowledging the Christ in the criminal, that may be because we would rather deny the Christ in ourselves. Denial is easier than acknowledging our own greatness and mercy, for that carries a responsibility to extend to ourselves and others, love and compassion.

The ultimate injustice is to treat a person as a non-person. To treat him in this way is, effectively, to say that he simply does not count as a human being. It is to deny the intrinsic worth of every human being created in God's image and likeness. It is a failure to see past the crime to the person of the criminal.

I have met no "animals" or "beasts" or "monsters" in prison. The famous Roscommon priest, Fr Flanagan, founder of Boy's Town in Omaha, Nebraska, had a great slogan, "There's no such thing as a bad boy". He was absolutely right. There are boys who do bad things, adults who do evil things, but we mustn't get the person and behaviour mixed up, for they are separate. How many of us can make that fine distinction? It is very easy to pronounce wholesale condemnation on both the person and his behaviour without distinguishing between the two. The easiest speech in the world is the condemnatory one.

LOVING SINNER, HATING SIN

A person guilty of rape said to me, "What do you think of rape?" I said, "Rape is a terrible crime. For the victim, it is worse than murder, because with murder the victim is dead. He is gone. The family must deal with it, but not the victim. Rape is worse. The victim has a lifetime of coping, of trying to understand, of asking questions, of knowing that the rapist is still alive and may someday escape or be released. Every hour of every day the victim relives it, step by step, minute by minute, and it hurts just as bad."

He said, "What does that make me out to be?" I said, "Rape is a hateful crime, but that does not make you a hateful person. There is a difference between who I am and what I do, between the sin and the sinner. I am not the crime I commit. I am more than the crime. I am more than my sin. I love the sinner but I hate the sin."

GOLDEN RULE

A sense of justice allows for anger and outrage. We integrate anger into love when we say, "I will not treat you the way you treat me." Otherwise, we are no better. People confuse forgiveness with condoning. There is no condoning the sheer evil of what the two convicted boys did to little James Bolger.

We can be redeemed. We can change our behaviour, repent, confess our sin, accept full responsibility, make amends, receive forgiveness and start again. We do not consign anyone to the dustbin. This is the more enlightened way. The other, alas, more travelled way, leads to chaos and anarchy.

It is a law of life that when we approach a human being as a person, with courtesy and respect, there is no telling what inner beauty we may find.

6 Prison Chaplain

Goethe said that you must put your head deep into the life around you, and what you bring up will have some truth in it.. This is what I would like to do in sharing with you the rather special work of prison chaplaincy.

Someone once said that 90% of living is about just showing up. Prison chaplains are good at showing up every day. We show up on the landings, in the yards, in the workshops, in the punishment pads, in the cells. We're available. We're there for anyone who needs us. We're there to recognise the individual, we call him by name, to recognise that he is something more than a number, a prisoner, a problem, a threat. We are there to protect whatever rights he has, to speak up for those who cannot speak up for themselves. We are there to show respect, to give the prisoner space to be himself, to tell his story. We're there to allow him to vent his anger against the system, the government and the Church, at our expense.

WE'RE THERE

We go to the cells, landings, yards, workshops, recreational areas, where the men and women are, accepting them as they are, encouraging all the response of which they are capable. It may be to show compassion rather than revulsion, forgiveness not blame, it may be to phone the Ma or the girlfriend to tell them that John is alright, or to phone Temple Street Hospital to find out how his kid is doing, or write a letter for someone who is illiterate. One such man confided, "I love the way you tell the missus I love her"!

It may be to allow yourself to be made use of and not mind too much. It may be to be told in very brief blunt language to go away. It may be to challenge his past, to point the way forward. It may be to treat the prison officers as well as you treat the prisoners, and see no incongruity. It may be to put your reputation on the line and to fail and be misunderstood. It may be to work to change the way prisoners are, and the way society perceives them to be. In short, it may be to try and do the 101 things that men and women deprived of their liberty cannot do for themselves.

INADEQUATE

What makes prison chaplaincy so difficult is that, even though I am in prison every day, I don't know what it's like to have my freedom taken away. I don't know what it's like to be a father separated from wife and children. I don't know what it's like to be locked up 16 hours a day. I don't eat prison food. I don't wear prison clothes. I have never been body-searched. I cannot look into a prisoners body and feel his pain. I can go home at the end of the day and visit my family and enjoy a round of golf, and do many of the wonderful things we, who enjoy freedom, can do and take so much for granted. But I see the damage these deprivations do and because I can do so little about it, I feel, most of the time, inadequate and powerless.

There are, of course, some terrific moments like the letter we received from an Englishman thanking us for being family to him during his long lonely years in prison. Like the young woman who said, "You made me feel I was something. I always thought of myself as dirt." Or the man who said, "You convinced us that we weren't second class citizens." Or the simple words of the prisoner in the isolation cell, "Thanks for dropping in, I feel better now."

SCHOOL OF LIFE

Prison Chaplaincy is a great learning experience. I have learned one of life's great truths, that the last thing we ever learn about ourselves is the effect we have on others. I have learned more about forgiveness: that no one is beyond the pale, no one is beyond redemption. I have learned that we would forgive most things if we knew all the facts. I learned from the man in the padded cell who told me he was glad he would be judged by God and not by man.

I have learned about not being judgmental. That none of us is good enough to throw the first stone. I think it was Kipling who said that if the Horseman came into the town at the dead of night and shouted "Flee, you've been found out." the whole town would be deserted the following morning. I subscribe to that view.

A LISTENER

I have learned the importance of listening and not talking. I remember the man who said "There were times when I thought I needed a psychiatrist; what I really needed was someone who would just listen to me." I have learned not to be naive and believe everything I read in the newspapers. I have learned not to personalise rejection. I realise that, more often than not, the way people treat me has more to do with them than with me. I find this insight liberating.

POSITION OF TRUST

Chaplaincy is a position of trust. Unless we are trusted by the men and women in prison we have no business there. Prisoners know that whatever passes between us is sacred, that we would never betray a trust or confidence. Sometimes the chaplain is the only real friend a prisoner allows himself.

Chaplaincy is about being faithful: not giving up on our commitments to the men and women in prison. Our presence saying: "You can rely on us." We won't always be perfect but we will be there for you. We won't walk away. What the chaplain wants to hear most from prisoners is: "They never gave up on us even when we gave up on ourselves. They believed in us even when we gave up on ourselves. They stayed with us even when we weren't worth staying with. They were there for us when we wanted them . . "

Prisoners are the lost sheep of the gospel, the men and women upon whom the man from Nazareth, Jesus of Galilee, set so much value, and said we must go out and find. But try telling that to prisoners, the chances are they won't believe you. It's better, safer, if the realisation creeps up, unnoticed

and surprises them. Much better if they make the God con-
nection themselves, with a little bit of help from chaplains. I
talk religion if a prisoner brings it up. Whether or not He is
invited, I know God will be there, in every greeting and ges-
ture and conversation we have. Ultimately, that's what matters.

CHERRY BLOSSOM TREE

It was at Easter when I noticed it for the first time. A
small Cherry Blossom tree in full bloom. It was growing in
the tiny flower garden in the women's prison. A young
offender was watering it. I asked her where the tree came
from. she told me that in January, as she was returning to the
prison after a family visit, she passed a skip full of garbage
and saw the tiny shrub lying on top of it.

She got permission to pick it up and plant it. Then each
day she tended the abandoned shrub and lovingly nursed it
back to life, and at Easter it blossomed for the first time.

I see in that Cherry Blossom tree an image of the prisoner, so often abandoned and dumped on the scrap heap of life,
waiting for someone with eyes to see, waiting to be salvaged
and planted again, and given the chance to grow and blossom and live again. I see, too, in that Cherry Blossom an
image of what a prison chaplain is called to be.

So each day we prison chaplains plant a seed and hope it
will fall on good soil, and that at some stage our influence
will be felt, that it may mean something, that it may make a
difference. Then we leave the rest to God.

7 Sea of Stress

Prison is a sea of stress. Everyone is in crisis. No one wants to be there. People ask me all the time "What is it like being a prison chaplain? How do you work in a place that does no good for people?" The obvious answer is that chaplains are not there because of the place. Who wants to be in prison anyway? We're there because of the people in that awful place. It's the people who make it worthwhile.

I'm frequently asked, "How do you survive? How do you cope? What keeps you going when you look into the eyes of someone you care for and his eyes tell you , 'I'm not going to make it?'"

BURN-OUT FACTOR

When you are dealing daily with AIDS, schizophrenia, depression and family breakdown, you are investing in the people you meet. It's exhausting because you are taking on a lot of pain. So the difficulties and pressures are not to be underestimated. Nevertheless, I think they can be overstated. If you know why you do what you are doing, have a vision, a sense of purpose, the commitment and the good sense not to take yourself too seriously, I think you can go into any situation and be effective. It's when you don't know why you do what you are doing and lack vision, you tend then to rush in where angels fear to tread, and end up in trouble, get hurt, break down and burn-out.

I'm not into success or fulfilment or making the world a better place. I find that approach to people too individualistic and self-centred. I accept my limitations, I am not a saviour. I may be a child of God but I am not God!

BLAME

I believe in personal responsibility. So, when my friend Tony died in a shoot-out, it wasn't I who lost him. I don't blame myself. I don't blame God or the Church or the Government or Society or the stars. I feel great sadness and a deep personal loss that one so young, talented, charming, full of potential and unfulfilled dreams, should die as he did in such a terrible way.

I did the best I could for him. I am not alone in what I do. I handed him over to God completely. The pain of loss may not go away at once. But this response enables me to cope, and stay intact, carry on with life, move on to the next person, and try to be as present to him as best I can.

If I blame myself for actions which are clearly not my fault, I rob myself of self-esteem and the capacity to act. If I blame myself entirely for someone's failure, downfall, death, that is a sign of excessive guilt. I am assuming a power over life and death which I do not possess.

DETACHMENT

I cultivate detachment. Detachment means letting go of the desire to save a particular person and the need to justify my existence in helping people. It means letting go, too, of dependence on my own gifts and insights in redeeming someone. If I really care, the greatest gift I can give another human being is the space to be himself, not tie him down unduly but leave him free to grow, experiment, make decisions, make mistakes and even to die. If however, care and concern fills me with self-doubt and anguish when someone I give myself to fails, then it is my needs not his that are being met. I am simply using him to satisfy my ego and need for success.

So I try not to over-invest in my person. I try not to take on too much responsibility. I try to be caring but careful. That kind of insight only comes with too many years of trying and failing and more pain than I ever want to think about.

COPING

There is of course much more to living in a stressed filled situation. I realise only too well that all such work and no play makes Jack a bad boy. Indeed, before I can take care of others, I must first take care of myself. People who fly have heard the announcement before take-off, or read it in the pocket literature, stating, if you are travelling with a small child and the cabin begins to lose pressure, take the oxygen yourself first and then take care of the baby.

When I first heard the announcement, I was somewhat surprised. It was alien to everything I had been taught and believed. "Me first?" I was taught that in a crisis, its women and children first. But after a little reflection, the reason for the directive became obvious. Only, if you can save yourself, can you save the helpless child. Looking after yourself and nourishing personal needs is also a basic requirement in life.

END OF THE DAY

At the end of a day in Mountjoy, I listen to the great gate closing. I leave the prison behind me. I know if I take it home I'll be torn apart. I walk down the avenue and away from it all. I thank God for freedom and the capacity to live life as fully as I can. I move gently to the next phase of life. I join a supportive community in St Saviours for the evening meal. I visit my family once or twice a week. I relax in their presence and enjoy the company of nieces and nephews and close friends.

But most evenings I am at home. If the day has been very demanding I spend some time watching dumb movies on television, preferably ones with the good guys winning, or else I listen to the classics or do some reading. I switch off. I unwind. I have developed a bad memory so that I can sleep at night. At the end of the day I pray for the young prodigals not yet returned to their Father, and not yet aware of their need for forgiveness. I pray for myself because I know, only too well, that but for the grace of God there go I.

8 Why More Prisons?

Our prison population is growing all the time. There has been a 75% increase over the past decade. The current jail population is 43% higher than that recommended by the Whitaker report in 1985. The Government's response has been to declare an all out attack against crime. The anti-crime package provides 210 prison spaces at a capital cost of £25m. Provision is to be made for 150 male offenders and 60 female offenders.

However, on the very day the Minister for Justice announced the law and order plans in Dail Eireann, Mountjoy prison, the States biggest jail, was over crowded; 187 prisoners were on temporary release and 250 prisoners were unlawfully at large.

MORE GARDAI?

The Minister also announced that the government will sanction a recruitment drive to allow an intake to the Garda College of 350 members per year for 1995-1997. Logically, extra gardai should result in better crime detection, more convictions and inevitably, greater demands for cell spaces for an ever increasing prison population.

By 1997, the revolving door will still be revolving at an even more alarming rate, the prison system will be in even worse chaos, and the Justice Minister of the day will be under intense public pressure to build more prisons and put more gardai on the streets.

A SOFT OPTION

Against a background of rising crime and a more frightened public, the demand for more jails and gardai is a gut reaction to our growing fears and anxieties. The obvious reason why we put people who break the law into prison, is to prevent and reduce crime. If, however, prison does neither, then we have to think more seriously about spending £66m. which is the total cost of the Minister's comprehensive law and order package. After all, if imprisonment were an effective way of preventing or even reducing crime, we should be blessed with a significantly lower crime rate. Not so. All the available evidence suggests that locking people up is a soft option with a miserable record of failure. Alarmingly, around 70 per cent of inmates offend again within two years of release. It would seem that if sending someone to jail is meant to discourage further criminal activity, it doesn't work.

No one is arguing that the criminal should not be punished. Prisoners themselves have a saying: "Don't do the crime, unless you can do the time." No one disputes that prisons are a necessary component of the criminal justice system.

SCHOOL OF CRIME

At the same time it must be said that prison today has little or no rehabilitative effect. No one who has visited a prison, with perception, can fail to be moved by the reality that they are places of hopelessness and degradation. Indeed, the argument about prisons as schools of crime is well known.

For imprisonment to deter offenders and potential offenders, it must be both a stigma and a punishment. The fear of prison, the shame it would bring to one's family and good name in the community, and the danger of being excluded from a group one cares about, undoubtedly, acts as a deterrent for most of us. But many of the imprisoned live in areas where their peers and, indeed, relatives have also done time. So the stigma attached may not be as great as when imprisonment was relatively uncommon. So going to prison holds less loss of 'social standing'. It doesn't frighten them any more. Of course, it's a very horrible experience. In the past, too, the real sanction was that if you'd been in prison it affected your job prospects. Now that doesn't apply. There aren't jobs anymore.

PRISON: A LAST RESORT

Prison does not work. It should be imposed not as a first option but as a last resort. Less use should be made of prison for those guilty of non-violent crimes, and far more use should be made of punishing them in non-custodial ways.

In this country there has never been a strong body of opinion in favour of a sentencing policy designed to be corrective. We go down the road of custodial sentences. If it deters others well and good, if not, then at least it will teach him a lesson. There has to be a better way than simply teaching a lesson, getting them off the streets, giving the public a break.

I realise that this point of view is cold comfort to someone whose car has been stolen, home burgled, or handbag snatched.

Building more jails will not make us safer. More prisons and harsher punishment won't make criminals think twice before they act. Tough talk does not stop criminals from re-offending.

We ask too much of prison. Our expectations of what imprisonment can achieve must be lowered. Our expectations of what social and educational programmes can do must be raised. We are left with the nagging question, is the Minister's vast £66m. proposed expenditure on crime money down the drain?

9   A Different Prison System

The prison system in this country has an alarming failure rate. Almost 70% offend within two years of release. In addition the cost of running the prisons last year was £108, 000,000 (One hundred and eight million pounds).

It is a lot of money for such a poor return. Schools and Hospitals recording this level of failure would be closed down. Any business organisation running at this loss would be declared bankrupt.

WHAT DO WE WANT?

This state of affairs prompts some pertinent questions: What kind of prison system do we want? One that punishes for the sake of punishing or offers the opportunity for reform and rehabilitation or includes both? It is only in asking the right questions that we can break out of a restrictive and unimaginative view of prison that is, unfortunately, all too pervasive today.

Speaking very broadly we may divide the prison population into two groups: violent and non-violent. Interestingly, the violent make up a mere 10 per cent. Yet, whenever we debate crime and punishment, particularly one inspired by some callous and vicious attack on an innocent person, the distinction between violent and non-violent becomes blurred. It's the violent who dominate the debate. We ignore the fact that one-third of the people committed to Mountjoy Prison are road traffic offenders. We insist on treating all prisoners the same, as we clamour for a tougher criminal justice that will push more people inside for longer sentences.

NOT ALL ARE EQUAL

I think we need to focus more on the 90 per cent behind bars who are not guilty of violent crimes. Men and women sentenced to six months or less do not constitute a threat to the general public. Yet the current practice in our Courts is to impose the ultimate sanction of prison and then to house all prisoners, violent and non-violent, under the same roof and subject to the same harsh conditions and regime.

Under the circumstances, is it any surprise that the prison system does not work? It doesn't make sense to mix professional and non professional, serious and non serious offenders. It's not uncommon to hear a young offender claim: "I have learned everything I know about crime in prison. It has made me what I am today."

PRISON CONDEMNS

Prison doesn't work because everything about it speaks of failure. A man is sent there against his will because in the eyes of society he is a failure. Every prison rule and regulation (and they are numerous) are negative statements saying, "You're no good, you're a criminal, we don't trust you." The longer he is there the more he accepts the characterisation and becomes what people say he is. It's a miracle when anyone emerges from this environment with any degree of self-respect and confidence.

The few, who come out unscathed by the experience, are classical examples of the human spirit – good triumphing over evil, and the capacity of ordinary people to rise to great heights.

But one swallow does not make a summer. Those who survive are the best. But it is totally unfair to ask a person to fight all the odds. If someone fights the odds and wins, you proclaim that person a champion. That's what medals are for. But you cannot ask the normal run-of-the-mill person to fight up-stream like a salmon, in a system that is programmed for failure.

ANTI-PRISONERS

Moreover, the anti-social stance we take against the imprisoned exacerbates the problem facing those who would wish to put the past behind them and turn over a new leaf. The famous line from Gone With the Wind, "Frankly, my dear Scarlet, I don't give a damn." can, in all fairness, be applied to our negative attitudes. We don't give a damn about prison or prisoners. We don't want to know these people. We are pleased to see them locked up, and then conveniently forget all about them.

VOICES OF THE UNHEARD

Prisons are not a political issue. They only become one when something serious happens; a prison riot or the destruction of prison property, or a violent confrontation between inmates and staff. We do not understand why the imprisoned behave in such a senseless manner. We see what happens but rarely ask why it happened. We fail to understand that riots are the voices of the unheard.

Life behind bars is brutalising. Any notion of personal responsibility is seriously diminished. You do as you are told when you are told. You lose most of the control over your life. Decisions are made, orders are given and a paramilitary structure implements the orders.

Life is a bore. Everyday is the same. It kills the spirit. It wrecks personal relationships. Drugs are available. Many inmates use drugs to escape the boredom and confinement.

A FAULTY PENAL SYSTEM

One of the most frequent phrases heard from sentencing Judges is that the sentence will deter others from offending. Everyone in prison knows that this is simply a myth. At fault is our penal system. It is based on a philosophy of retributive justice. A system built on negativity can only produce negative results.

Many good programmes tried over the years have been conducted within the negative framework of punishment, containment and lack of trust. You cannot punish and reconcile at the same time. Contradictory objectives can only lead to a stalemate or total paralysis. This is not a question of ideology. It is simply a question of logic.

JUSTICE: RETRIBUTIVE

Retributive justice has brought nothing but chaos and distress to the people caught up in it. It has guaranteed a growing level of crime and wasted millions in taxpayers money . We need to discover a philosophy that moves from punishment to reconciliation, vengeance against offenders to healing victims, from alienation to integration. That philosophy base is restorative justice.

JUSTICE: RESTORATIVE

Retributive justice asks: "How do we punish this offender"?

Restorative justice asks: "How do we restore the well-being of the victim, the community and the offender?" What we need are not more prisons, but a different prison system. Indeed, to embark on a building programme of new prisons without first addressing the shortcomings of the retributive system, appears to me to be misguided and counter-productive.

10 *Dead Man Walking*

No opinion poll has been taken in Ireland on capital punishment, but poll after poll in America and the U.K. has indi-
cated widespread support for putting violent criminals to
death. If such a poll were taken in this country, I believe the
majority would support the death penalty.

Of course, crime is a terrible problem, and more must be
done to stop the violence, but I do not believe that killing,
sanctioned by the State, is the answer.

DEVALUING LIFE

Capital punishment is the taking of life. Every time we
deliberately take a human life, the life of a tiny unborn baby,
the life of an A.I.D.S. victim, the lives of little children, young
women, old men, we blunt ourselves to the sacredness of all
human life.

There is, of course, a radical difference between taking an
innocent life and taking the life of someone who has been
tried and found guilty, beyond a shadow of doubt, of murder. Indeed, those who favour the death penalty in certain
cases, argue that it is precisely to protect the innocent life that
the murderer should be executed. It is, perhaps, on this
point that opposing sides differ most of all. Those who reject
capital punishment argue that executing a murderer for taking an innocent life, simply does not protect innocent lives.
It simply does not have this effect.

What then motivates those who argue in favour of capital punishment if they have no guarantee that killing a murderer will save anyone else in the future? Is it frustration? Is
it anger? My loved one is dead, dead at the hands of a murderer. No one can bring back my love. No one can fill this
terrible loneliness and emptiness in my soul. I am a mother,
a father, they have killed my daughter, my son. I am a husband, a wife, they have killed my 'other half'. I am a widow,

who will support me? Who will help me rear my children?

A LIFE FOR A LIFE

At the same time, hundreds of millions of pounds change hands in drug traffic. Drugs are pushed publicly. Lives are destroyed, hearts broken, families torn apart and the police apparently are unable to stop the destruction.

In other words, I can be killed, my daughter raped, my children mutilated and I have no defence. The system, whether corrupt or indifferent or incompetent, doesn't seem to work. I can't stand it. I won't accept it. Someone must be punished. I must have justice for what has been done to me and my family. I can accept nothing less than a life for a life.

Who can't understand that anger of frustration? I, for one, have buried murder victims. I have known their loved ones. I have visited people paralysed for life because of murderous intent. I have, also, for 6 years, worked closely with people who have committed murder. I can see, too, that far too little is done for the victims of violence. I can understand why people call for the death penalty. I can understand the almost primitive cry for help against future crime and the help people think they see in capital punishment.

LIFE IS PRECIOUS

I am not convinced, however, that killing someone, who killed someone, is the way to show that killing is wrong. We cannot compensate for the taking of one life by the taking of another. There has to be a more civilised way to deter violence.

There are no easy solutions to crime, but the death penalty, in my view, aggravates rather than solves the problem.

VIOLENCE IS THE PROBLEM

I believe we have become obsessed with violence as the only solution to violence. This is to give up on ourselves. We need to recognise that violence itself is the problem, and the more we resort to it, the worse we make it.

We fool ourselves when we think we are getting tough on crime and getting at its roots by executing criminals. Just look at the evidence. Just look at the relatively few people who are doing life sentences in comparison with the thousands of increasing violent crimes.

A MOTHER'S TESTIMONY

Recently, on one of the afternoon talk shows on television, a mother, whose young daughter had been raped and murdered, expressed the most eloquent position on the death penalty I have heard.

She said that her daughter was very precious. She felt the best way to honour her was not to kill someone in her name, but to say that all life is sacred and worthy of preservation. She stated that she was a Christian and felt that the concept of capital punishment violates a mandate of forgiveness for which she is going to be held accountable. No amount of retaliatory deaths were going to compensate for the value of her daughter's life.

Even in the current climate, it is hard to believe that there are people created by God who are beyond saving, that there are persons not worth the effort it would take to restore them to true humanity.

LOVE AND FORGIVENESS

Many assume that the Bible supports the death penalty. The only problem with this argument is that the Bible calls for death, not only for acts of murder, but also for adultery, fornication, blasphemy, and other sins. If one were to literally apply the code of Biblical law, there would be few people to carry out the prescribed executions. In the process we would miss out on the central message of love and forgiveness in the New Testament.

QUICK FIX

More and more, society has been coming up with quick fixes, and they are increasingly violent. Death becomes the quick fix. Instead of dealing with the problems of the sick and elderly, one response is "just kill them". No more argument. No more discussion.

I would never condemn anyone for having an abortion, but I would say it was wrong. It is a quick fix. The death penalty (like abortion, euthanasia, and assisted suicides) lulls us into thinking we are solving the problems of society. But what have we solved? What we have done is to have, generally, accepted violence as a way of life.

The death penalty is a symbol of a society giving up. Giving up, not only on the individual, but, on life itself. It is an admission that the only answer we have to crime and violence is to exercise a policy of an eye for an eye, a death for a death.

11 Farewell Mountjoy

The French have a saying, "Each time we say good-bye we die a little." If that is true then I died a 'little' on August 31st 1995, the last day of a six year chaplaincy with, I must add, no time off for good conduct!

THE SONG HAS ENDED

I covered every yard of the prison that Thursday. And there was no lack of friendly advice. One of the long term prisoners echoed the sentiments of many when he advised me to get on with my life and forget the so-and-so place. I knew leaving the place would be easy, but hard leaving behind the men and women I knew so well in that awful place we call prison.

THE MELODY LINGERS ON

It was lock-up time in the late afternoon when I made it back to the office. The prison was quiet. Everyone was present and accounted for. I cleared the desk, filed some letters, emptied the waste paper basket, and tidied up for my successor who was starting the following morning. I sat on the chair for a few moments. There was time for one last little 'think'. The window was open. I could see the great forbidding gates of Mountjoy Prison. I remembered the first time I passed through them. It was in the spring of '79. I was parish priest of inner Tallaght. I visited parishioners on Thursday mornings, and afterwards made the one mile journey to my old home on Caragh Road to spend the remainder of the day with my elderly parents. It was during those weekly visits to Mountjoy that I developed a feeling for prison ministry and now, 16 years later, as I gazed out the windows, I realised that for 6 years I had been doing something I always wanted to do.

Now it was time to leave it all behind. So I let down the window, gathered my bits and pieces, closed the door, handed in the key, crossed the yard for the last time, had a brief word with the officer at the gate and stepped outside. When the steel gate closed, a significant chapter of my life closed with it.

I walked away slowly but not without looking back.

DANNY!

On my way to the Dominican Priory, St Saviours, a mere 10 minutes walk, I passed the taxi rank opposite the Mater Hospital and remembered Danny (not his real name). He was a prisoner-patient, seriously ill with an A.I.D.S. related condition. He was, in prison terms, a 'heavy' and under 24 hours guard. He made a bid for freedom by jumping from an upstairs window. He made it alright to the taxi-rank but, unfortunately for him, his escape was spotted by prison officers returning from lunch and he was quickly recaptured. He was, in due course, discharged from hospital and returned to Mountjoy to serve the balance of his sentence. But his health continued to deteriorate, causing grave concern. He was passed for a release programme by the Department of Justice allowing him a series of A.M. to P.M. home visits in the company of the Chaplain.

MEMORIES

On the first visit, he asked me to drive through the Phoenix Park, a place he referred to, as his neck of the woods. When we passed the famous Wellington Monument he expressed the wish to make the climb, for old time's sake. He raced on ahead and as I approached, looked down, opened wide his arms in triumph, and cried out at the top of his voice, "I'm free". He beckoned me to join him. We sat on the top step and surveyed the scene below. He was completely at home. This was his territory, the playing field where he spent much of his happy-go-lucky childhood. He took great pleasure pointing out the well known landmarks. He observed with a sense of wonder how green the grass was. He counted the magpies, and envied the young couples walking hand in hand.

He talked about the past, regretted the lifestyle that killed the dream he once dreamed, regretted, too, the pain and hurt caused to innocent people. He wished he could undo the harm done;

wished, too, he could turn the clock back and start again.

FOOTPRINTS

Danny could neither read nor write, but he had a good memory and "Footprints" was one of his favourite pieces. Then completely out of the blue he began to recite the poem and it sounded differently because he made the words his own.

> "One night a man had a dream. He dreamed he was
> walking along the beach with the Lord . . . He noticed
> only one set of footprints at times . . . . and it happened
> at the lowest and saddest times in his life . . . . and it
> bothered him . . . and he questioned the Lord . . . and the
> Lord replied, my precious child, when you see one set of
> footprints, it was then that I carried you."

When he finished there was silence, it was as if time stood still, neither of us daring to speak, each wanting the precious moment to last forever. It was one of those rare times that come too infrequently in life when, oblivious of our surroundings, we become aware of a greater presence.

CRY FREEDOM

Danny was released from prison a few months later on T.R (temporary release). He came home to die. He knew the end was near and time running out. He wasn't looking forward to much but dreaded the thought of dying in custody. Happily, the Minister of Justice granted his dying wish and ordered full release on compassionate grounds. I sat on the corner of his bed and witnessed the signing of the release form. It was a very special moment for him. He raised it high above his head like a trophy, and with eyes gleaming, turned to his mother and said, "Ma, I'm free, I'm really free now!" Not too long afterwards, the Lord called him, and this time he was free, free at last. But not before gently reminding me that what matters, is not what we do for others, but rather what they do for us.

THANKS FOR THE MEMORIES

On the wall behind the bed, there was a Jimmy Hendrix poster. There was a quotation on it. It said simply: "When I die keep playing my records." Today, I play Danny's record in honour of the many young, and not so young, men and women who enriched my life during six long years behind grey walls and barred windows of Mountjoy Prison.

Indeed, when I look over my life and remember the places I lived in and the people I met, I think the thing that makes the deepest impression on me is that people are the same everywhere. We have the same basic needs and desires, the same worries and fears, the same dreams and hopes.

My next pastoral assignment takes me to Western Canada to work amongst the Asian Community. What the future holds is yet to unfold. Whatever it may be, I will remember Mountjoy and the day 'I died a little', when we said our last good byes.